BUDDHIST CHARACTER ANALYSIS

Robert Mann and **Rose Youd** were among the first students to seek instruction at the House of Inner Tranquillity, a Buddhist meditation centre which was founded by Alan and Jacqui James in Bradford on Avon, Wiltshire, in 1980.

The following year, Robert moved into the centre as full-time trainee and personal assistant to the teachers. In 1987 he was appointed assistant teacher. Today, he also plays a central role in the management and administration of the House of Inner Tranquillity and its two associated monasteries.

Rose ordained as a nun at the Monastery of Infinite Compassion when it opened in 1988. Since 1989, as senior nun, she has been teaching and lecturing both at the centre itself and at its satellite group in London.

BUDDHIST CHARACTER ANALYSIS

Robert Mann & Rose Youd

AUKANA   Bradford on Avon

Reprinted 1995
First published in 1992

Aukana Trust,
9 Masons Lane, Bradford on Avon, Wiltshire BA15 1QN
The Aukana Trust is a registered charity (No 326938)

Copyright © Aukana Trust 1992

Cover photograph by Robert Mann

Printed in Great Britain by Redwood Books, Trowbridge
Cover printed by Devenish & Co, Bath

British Library Cataloguing in Publication Data
Mann, Robert
  Buddhist Character Analysis
  1. Buddhism – Doctrines
  I. Title   II. Youd, Rose
  294.3

  ISBN 0-9511769-3-5

ACKNOWLEDGEMENTS

Alan and Jacqui James, whose lectures and teachings on the classification of character types formed the catalyst for this book

Bhikkhu Bodhi and the **Buddhist Publication Society** of Kandy, Sri Lanka, for permission to quote from Bhikkhu Ñanamoli's translation of the *Visuddhi-Magga* and from Bhikkhu Nyanatiloka's *Buddhist Dictionary*

The Pali Text Society, for permission to quote from their copyright translations of the Pali Canon

Garry Phillipson, for editorial suggestions, advice and assistance

Derek Fuller, for typographical assistance

Michael Phoenix, for permission to use the cover photograph

CONTENTS

Dedicated with gratitude to our teacher, Alan James

WHY IT DOESN'T NEED CHARACTER ANALYSIS

1

WHY BUDDHIST CHARACTER ANALYSIS?

*There are two kinds of people in the world: those who divide the
world into two kinds of people, and those who do not –
Robert Benchley*

Throughout the ages, the grouping of people into types has
been a favourite human occupation and literally hundreds of
different systems have come into being. The criteria on which
they have been based vary considerably, ranging from the
physiological and psychological, through the socio-economic,
to the philosophical and religious. All manner of scientific or
quasi-scientific schemes have emerged, from the sophisticated
to the simplistic.

In the West one of the earliest forms of analysis was that of
Hippocrates, whose division of human beings into two types
was based on body shape. Aristotle formulated several
systems according to what he considered to be people's
primary psychological motivations. More recently, Nietzsche

categorised people into Dionysian and Apollonian types. Other classificatory schemes devised in modern times include those of Marx, Freud, Jung and Eysenck. From the occult tradition other systems have originated, perhaps the best known being that of astrological types.

There are also, of course, many systems to be found in non-Western cultures, such as the five-element matrix of traditional Chinese medicine. As Robert Benchley's remark implies, the number is potentially infinite.

Many, if studied and applied correctly, are both accurate and effective. They're accurate in that the lines of approach they suggest can be seen to correspond with our actual day-to-day experience of people and how they behave; effective in that they can lead to a greater understanding of others and of ourselves. All of them are arbitrary – human beings are too complex and, more pertinently, too changeable for any system to even come close to being absolute.

Given its love of classification and analysis, it's hardly surprising to find that Buddhism contains within it a system of character types. But as there are already so many others to choose from, why do we need Buddhist character analysis? Why bring in yet another approach? In the first place, this particular approach is far from new – in fact its foundations were laid over twenty-five centuries ago. But most importantly, whilst other systems can most certainly deepen our wisdom about life as a human being among other human beings, that's as far as they go.

Buddhist character analysis goes further. It promises greater insight into human behaviour, yes – but when taken in its proper context, not only does it lead towards a deeper understanding of the vagaries of the human personality but it also forms an integral part of the route towards the solution of the profoundest questions about life and its purpose. You can, after all, become as wise and as knowledgeable as you like about people but that wisdom will do nothing to unravel the mysteries of birth and death. The Buddhist classification of character types need not be an end in itself – if used correctly, it becomes an invaluable aid in coming to that total understanding which is known as enlightenment.

* * *

For anyone wishing to become an outstanding teacher in whatever sphere an essential requirement is a shrewd and subtle understanding of human behaviour. The Buddha, one of the most successful spiritual teachers the world has known, was no exception.

Born in 566 BCE as heir to the throne of a small kingdom on the Indian borders of present-day Nepal, Siddhattha Gotama spent the first twenty-nine years of his life in the lap of royal luxury. Legend has it that shortly after his birth a prediction was made that the young prince would retire from the world and become a Buddha, one who reveals the way to spiritual awakening. His father, fearing to lose his successor, endeavoured to keep Siddhattha inside the royal estate, shielded from the dark side of life, the poverty, sickness, ageing and death that lay outside the palace gates.

The protective shield, however, could not be maintained: on a rare expedition into the town Siddhattha's eyes were opened to the facts when he encountered an old man, a sick man and a corpse. He also saw a recluse, one who has renounced the world to seek for truth, and was instantly inspired to abandon the pleasures of wealth and follow suit.

Enrolling as a student with two of the leading teachers of the day, the Buddha-to-be learned how to attain the deepest states of concentration. He soon became aware that an ability to control the mind was not enough to allay the sense of dissatisfaction he still felt. Going his own way, he tried the path of asceticism, mortifying his body until he was on the verge of death. Still he found no peace.

Then one night, seated under an *assattha* tree by the River Nerañjara, he discovered the path that lay between the extremes of indulgence and self-mortification, the middle way that is the way to enlightenment.

For the forty-five years that followed, the Buddha taught. He taught men, women, children; he taught the rich and the poor; he taught kings, priests, warriors, wanderers and slaves. Through his understanding of people and his consequent skill in relating with them, he was able to communicate his message throughout the whole spectrum of the Indian society of his day.

On one occasion, the Buddha enumerated the ten powers which entitled him to claim the foremost place among men (he called it roaring his lion's roar). Alongside his knowledge of his past lives, his consummate skill in meditation and his attainment of enlightenment itself, he included his ability to understand 'as they really are the divers characters of beings'. When he taught he always bore this diversity in mind, adapting his words to suit his audience. That so many were able to learn so much from his teaching is evidence of his ability to understand his students.

*   *   *

The Pali Canon (comprising forty volumes in the English translation) is a collection of the original teachings of the Buddha and forms the basis of the school of Buddhism known as Theravada; it's here that the Buddhist theory of character analysis has its origins. (For an account of character types in the Mahayana tradition see *Tso-ch'an San-mei Ching* by Sangharaksha.)

In the centuries following the Buddha's death the analysis underwent a process of expansion and evolution, and it makes its major appearance, fully systematised, in a commentarial work written in Sri Lanka in the fifth century CE: the Visuddhi-Magga, or Path of Purification, Bhadantacariya Buddha-ghosa's detailed overview of the Buddhist path.

The context in which character analysis is introduced is that of a monk seeking instruction in meditation. Buddhaghosa describes what sort of teacher the student should look for – ideally, one who has himself attained enlightenment. He explains how the student should approach the man he hopes to learn from with the correct attitude – not asking for instruction the moment he finds him but acting as his personal attendant for several days, until the teacher asks 'Why have you come?' Then the student may make his request for an appropriate meditation subject. There are many different kinds of meditation; the teacher will decide which kind will most benefit a specific pupil, Buddhaghosa tells us, by determining his particular temperament.

The system of character analysis he goes on to describe is not something which is commonly found in books written on Buddhism. Up until recent years Western interest in the Buddha's teaching has been largely academic, and this straightforward and very practical approach to analysis – relevant not only in the field of meditation but also in human relationships generally – rarely drew attention.

The description in the Visuddhi-Magga did not, however, escape the notice of Alan and Jacqui James, two of the pioneers in the field of Buddhist meditation in this country. The information given on character types by Buddhaghosa confirmed the conclusions they had drawn from their years of practising and teaching meditation. They continued to observe – not just meditators but people in general – and the observations they made served to strengthen their view that Buddhist character analysis is as effective and viable a scheme now as it was all those centuries ago.

People, after all, are basically much the same as they've always been, passing through the same kind of life experiences, motivated by the same kind of passions, ever caught up in the pursuit of pleasure and the avoidance of pain. Superficial circumstances may differ radically, in terms of the level of technology or education, the urban or agrarian nature of society, but human nature never really changes, and a twentieth-century fashion designer can be classified according to Buddhist character analysis just as readily as could an Oriental monk of ages past.

During their years of teaching, Alan and Jacqui James not only validated the accuracy and effectiveness of the system as a whole but also became increasingly adept in translating the external clues that help to determine character type into modern terms, expanding and developing the system in accordance with their findings.

What Buddhist character analysis is and how it can be applied today is the subject of this book.

2

WHAT IS
BUDDHIST CHARACTER ANALYSIS?

Mind is the forerunner of all things, mind is foremost, of mind are all things made – Dhammapada, verse 1

The simplest division of human experience is that of mind and body, and according to Buddhist philosophy, it's mind that is dominant – it's our mental actions that condition what we do physically and verbally.

Buddhist character analysis distinguishes six fundamental movements of mind, six roots of behaviour. Just as a plant or tree will grow in dependence on its roots, so from each of these character-roots there grows up a whole set of mental, physical and verbal behaviour patterns. To determine which root is operative in any particular individual, either we can consider their typical states of mind, or we can work from the outside in: observing and categorising their outward behaviour to identify from which of the six it derives.

The six roots are: craving, hatred, confusion, faith, intelligence and speculation. These six condition everything we do – from our thinking patterns to the way we walk down the street, to the things we decide to accumulate, to the friends we prefer to make, to the kinds of lifestyle we opt for. It must be emphasised that these roots are volitional. Craving and hatred are not things that just happen to us – we actually choose to do them, whether or not we are conscious of the fact.

The six roots can be grouped into three pairs: craving and faith; hatred and intelligence; confusion and speculation. Each pair represents the same basic principle, expressing itself either positively (faith, intelligence, speculation) or negatively (craving, hatred, confusion). Buddhism, taking a functional rather than a moral approach, does not describe the positive and negative as good and evil but chooses rather to identify actions as either efficient or inefficient.

Inefficient	*Craving*	*Hatred*	*Confusion*
Efficient	*Faith*	*Intelligence*	*Speculation*

Inefficient behaviour is that which is basically selfish, destructive of harmony, leading towards unpleasant results, towards pain. It includes, for instance, killing, stealing, lying, slander, envy, greed, conceit. The Buddha once described the link between the three inefficient or negative roots and suffering as follows:

Enraptured with craving, enraged with hatred, blinded by confusion, overwhelmed, with mind ensnared, man aims at his own ruin, at others' ruin, at the ruin of both, and he experiences mental pain and grief. He follows inefficient ways in deeds, words and thoughts, and he really knows neither his own welfare, nor the welfare of others, nor the welfare of both. These things make him blind and ignorant, hinder his knowledge, are painful, and do not lead him to peace – Anguttara Nikaya

Efficient behaviour, on the other hand, is unselfish, conducive to more harmonious living, leading towards pleasant results, towards a lessening of suffering, pain and distress. Helping others, service, generosity and compassion are examples of efficient action – as is restraint of the inefficient.

If we consider purely functional human behaviour (such as posture or preference in dress-style), because each pair of roots expresses the same basic principle, we only need to deal with the three pairs rather than the six individual roots. Thus when talking about external matters, the Visuddhi-Magga refers simply to the craver or craving type, the hate type and the confused type, implicitly including the positive roots in a convenient shorthand.

However, when we consider ethical behaviour – volitional mental responses – there is a vast difference between craving and faith types, hate and intelligent types, confused and speculative types. Actions rooted in craving, hatred and confusion are inefficient, whereas those rooted in faith, intelligence and speculation are efficient and as such reduce rather than increase suffering.

To take the first pair of roots: what craving and faith have in common is that they both want to acquire, to accumulate, to hold on unshakeably. Cravers hold on to the inefficient – that which, whether they know it or not, will in the long term lead to pain and distress. Faith types hold on to the efficient; they're reluctant to let go of things which are profitable, which lead towards greater happiness. It's the opposite end of the spectrum from craving but it's still the same trait operating, still the same basic thrust of behaviour: hanging on and not letting go.

For hatred and intelligence, the common characteristic is the desire to get rid of, destroy, do away with. Hate types want to get rid of everything: they have few possessions, few friends, few responsibilities. Intelligent types get rid of the inefficient factors in their life and lifestyle. While hate types get rid of things they don't like, intelligent types get rid of those things which are not to their benefit.

We can similarly align confused and speculative types. Confused types have no solid opinion about anything; they just want to follow the lead of somebody else. Speculative types also tend not to have fixed opinions, but in their case it's because they see so many possible options they just can't decide which is best. They've got a hundred and one different theories to entertain and they find it impossible to choose between them.

So both confused and speculative types are undecided: confused types are uncertain and do nothing about it – in fact they don't know what to do about it and just dither; speculative types also experience uncertainty but they try to solve it in some way. They're sure they've got the answer if only they could think it through one more time.

We can sum up these three spectra of behaviour quite simply (if rather simplistically): the craver says 'Yes please!'; the hate type, 'No thank you!'; and the confused type, 'Don't know.'

To put it another way, cravers overvalue everything – they place an unrealistic expectation of worth on whatever it is they desire; hate types undervalue everything – they say, 'It's not worth it – throw it away'; and in the case of confused types, ignorance is bliss.

It must be emphasised, however, that none of us is a pure type. There is no one who is purely a craver, purely a hate type, purely a confused type. Each of us has potentially present within our mental make-up a mixture of several – or indeed all – of the six roots, any one of which may be dominant at particular times and under particular circumstances.

We all change; there is no such thing as a static personality. At one time an individual may be full of anger and hatred – at such a time the hate root is prominent and expresses itself in certain distinctive kinds of behaviour. At another time he may be full of desire – then it is craving which is to the fore. If over a period of time, however, we judge that the subject of our analysis displays the root of hatred, for example, more often than he does the other five, then we classify such a person as a hate type. But the shorthand label of 'hate type' carries with it the understanding that whilst hatred may be dominant, any of the other roots may surface dependent on circumstances. Equally, it's quite possible for someone to display particular roots in very similar proportions, making them, say, a craving-speculative type or a hating-confused type.

To those of us who like to regard ourselves as infinitely complex, the idea of reducing human beings down into a mere six or even three types may seem simplistic. Yet it's an unquestionable fact, which can be verified by anyone who cares to take the trouble to observe, that there only actually exist variations on three basic movements of mind. When faced with an object, of whatever kind, we can only move towards it, move away from it or not know which way to move.

Buddhist character analysis is not, after all, a theoretical system, a construction of probabilities and possibilities based on someone's ideas of how things might work. Rather it is a very practical system, solidly grounded on the observation of human experience.

3

HOW TO ANALYSE CHARACTER

Before we go on to describe the way the roots of character
operate in more detail, we need to ask how it is that you
recognise a particular behaviour pattern, or which of the roots
is operative for a particular individual at any one time. There
are three possible approaches.

In the first place, you can quite simply ask. You can
question the person concerned about their behaviour patterns,
mental, physical and verbal, and make your deduction in
accordance with their replies. The major drawback to this
method is that it depends upon your subjects knowing
themselves well enough to provide you with the correct
information.

Secondly there is mind-to-mind contact or telepathy, direct
knowledge of another's mind. Of course, not everyone
believes that such a phenomenon exists, and the issue is
further clouded by those who believe they are telepathic and
yet are quite deluded. Buddhism, however, categorically

states that telepathy is a reality; moreover, it's an ability which anyone can develop if they're prepared to put in the work. If someone is truly skilled in this way, they'll be able to ascertain which roots are present without any difficulty whatsoever. It's certainly the surest method – its drawback is that those who have the capacity to use it are few and far between.

The most common method is that of observation and inference. In other words, you observe certain patterns of behaviour (traditionally, there are as we shall see seven particular aspects that are considered) and you infer from those patterns which of the roots must be present in the mind. Over a period of time you can thus build up a very accurate picture of a person's character.

It is important to stress that character analysis does take time – it's not possible to make instant assessments. For one thing, it takes time for anybody to familiarise themselves with the system. Whilst reading this book will provide you with the necessary information, it needs to be properly digested and assimilated by checking it against your own observation of those around you.

Further, it would be unwise even for someone thoroughly acquainted with the system to make a snap judgement about another's character. To assess a person as a hate type because they happen to be in an irritable frame of mind on the occasion you meet them would be ridiculously naïve.

We need to get a rounded balanced picture of our subjects, and that's only possible by having the patience to watch and wait, to observe over time. We can thus see them in both good moods and bad moods, both elated and depressed. We can judge for what proportion of the time they're displaying qualities of confusion or hatred or faith or intelligence. Consequently our assessments, when we do come to make them, will be based on a considerable quantity of information.

At first sight this form of analysis can seem deceptively simple. And yet the more we practise it, the more clearly we come to see the way the roots operate in all areas of life. Growing experience of the system will lead to an appreciation of its complexity, as it reveals layer upon layer of subtlety.

To use character analysis superficially is to misuse it. If you treat it as some kind of parlour game – going around analysing yourself and everybody else without any real knowledge of the scheme – you may well be inundated with volunteers for analysis; many people are fascinated by parlour games of a psychological nature. But unless you understand what you're doing, not only are you likely to draw wrong conclusions, but also you'll find that the type of insights you gain about people will be as superficial as your approach.

Assessment of character (whether one's own or another person's) using the Buddhist scheme requires a capacity for both analysis and synthesis. Good analysis depends upon accurate observation, the ability to observe what is actually present – rather than what you think is present, or what you would like to be present, or what you think ought to be present. Having amassed sufficient data, you then need to be able to form a coherent and integrated picture of the personality in question – this is the process of synthesis. If you don't have enough information, or if your original data are faulty in some way, then the assessment you make will be incomplete or inaccurate.

Another word of warning: it can be quite difficult to analyse yourself; it's usually easier to assess other people. Witness the way we can sometimes be very aware of and annoyed by another person's faults; yet it can take some while before we become prepared to admit that the faults we find so irritating in another are also our own.

Usually one of the first things a person does when they hear about analysis by character types is ask 'What type am I?' The next thing they do is analyse themselves and get it wrong. Not only does this method of assessment require the development of some degree of self-awareness (there are people, after all, who can be full of hatred or anger and yet blithely ignorant of that fact) but it also requires detachment and impartiality, qualities which are not always easy to maintain when we're looking at ourselves.

Perhaps we can see in ourselves moments of craving, moments of intelligence, moments of faith, moments of confusion – we seem to have a bit of every type of personality and it can be hard to see where the predominance falls. We may know ourselves well enough to recognise a mental state of, say, hatred quite clearly when it's present; but to judge in what proportions we habitually express the different roots can be tricky. A knowledgeable and unbiased observer can be of great assistance in guiding us towards an accurate assessment of our own character.

EXTERNAL SIGNS

The Visuddhi-Magga lists six different areas of physical behaviour
that can be used as a basis for observation: manner of dress, manner of
posture, manner of eating, manner of sleeping, manner of working
and manner of looking at objects.

When considering external behaviour, as we saw in Chapter 2, the
six roots of character can be reduced to three – the craving type and the
faith type share a similar approach, as do the hate and intelligent types
and the confused and speculative types. In the following chapters we'll
look at the way the different character types behave in each of the six
areas, using the shorthand of craving, hate and confused to include the
positive roots as well.

4

MANNER OF DRESS

*One of **craving temperament** wears his robe neither too tightly nor too loosely, confidently and level all round.*
*One of **hating temperament** wears it too tight and not level all round.*
*One of **confused temperament** wears it loosely and in a muddled way – Visuddhi-Magga*

Whilst the Visuddhi-Magga's analysis of dress refers specifically to the saffron robes of Buddhist monks, the principle expressed still applies whatever the culturally accepted style of clothing. It's just as valid for cravers, haters and confused types of the twentieth-century West as it was for the monks of Buddhaghosa's day.

When it comes to the appearance of **the craving type** of personality, the key-word is elegance. Cravers wear their clothes not too loose, not too tight – just so. The kind of colours they generally prefer are ones that are clean, pure, often bright. Clothes can be quite important to cravers – most of them like to be fashionable, although there are those among them who will disregard the latest trends, choosing rather to create a look which is all their own.

Whether their garments are tailor-made or bargains picked up from the local charity shop, they wear them with style. Sometimes it seems as if you could give them last year's flour sack to put on and they could make it look good; they have the dress-sense, the flair, to carry it off. It doesn't matter whether cravers are going to the theatre or mucking out the pigs: they invariably manage to look right.

And in keeping with the 'Yes please!' attitude to life of a craver, when it comes to clothes he or she has lots of them. Cravers operate on the principle that more equals better – they're forever going shopping, and if they're not careful they're likely to end up with wardrobes full of clothes they no longer like and dozens of pairs of shoes stashed away in odd corners that they don't know what to do with.

If the eye of a female craver is caught by a dress as she passes a shop window, she will find it very difficult to resist entering the shop and trying it on. Whilst she's in there, she'll probably be tempted to have a look at some other items as well. She's unlikely to be able to leave without making some kind of purchase.

Cravers can always find pressing reasons for acquiring whatever it is they currently desire. If accused of extravagance, they may well take pains to explain how very necessary their purchases are, and may even believe their own rationalisations.

In the case of **hate types**, one of the most noticeable features about their clothes is that they're generally worn too tight. The overall effect may be reasonably presentable but everything seems as though it's just a size too small. It's not because the hate type is overweight – far from it, as we'll see when we come to consider eating; it's just that they've a tendency to keep themselves under tension, mentally and physically. A hate type doing up shoelaces, for example, may tie the knot with real force, such that it will take considerable patience and dexterity to undo it.

The kind of colours a hate type prefers are retiring ones: muted browns, beiges, greys. They like to wear colours that don't attract attention – they aim at camouflage rather than display. The last thing hate types want is to be noticed. They want to be left alone to do their own thing with as little interference from other people as possible, which is quite the opposite of cravers, who like nothing better than to be the centre of attention – hence their bright colours and flamboyant styles.

Whilst the craver's attitude to shopping is 'Spend spend spend!', hate types will put off clothes-buying until it really is essential. Accordingly the clothes they do own may look as though they're wearing rather thin, and they'll probably occupy a couple of shelves rather than the craver's couple of wardrobes. Because hate types so rarely visit the shops, the style of their clothes is often somewhat dated. Not that being out of tune with fashion trends particularly bothers them; they're not very interested in people and don't much care what others think of them.

To present a parody of **the confused type** of personality: take such a person to a Savile Row outfitter's, buy him a £1,000 suit with all the accessories to match and get him dressed up in it so that he looks absolutely immaculate. Come back and check up on him half-an-hour later: he looks like he's been dragged through the proverbial hedge backwards. Collar points are askew; tie beginning to twist round his neck; trousers gone baggy at the knees; socks bunched round his ankles; shoe-laces untied and shoes scuffed. No one would now recognise that high-quality suit.

When the root of confusion is predominant, clothes are generally untidy, crumpled and dirty. Confused types frequently manage to spill something down their front; or maybe they'll sit down on a bench and get mud on their trousers or their pen leaks in their pocket. They notice none of this, quite unaware of all the minor accidents their clothes have undergone. Put a flour sack on a confused type and you probably wouldn't notice the difference.

Not surprisingly, the colours they choose to wear are muddy ones: muddy browns, muddy purples, muddy greens, muddy yellows. As they tend to put on the first garments they come across, oblivious as to whether or not they make a suitable combination, the items they select will often clash. A woman who wears a flimsy pastel-coloured summer dress, for example, with thick dark socks and heavy brogues shows signs of confusion. But just because someone's dressed in a mixture of yellow and cerise or orange and blue, that doesn't necessarily mean they're a confused type. Clashing colours draw the eye – such a 'Look at me!' message may be the conscious and deliberate choice of a craver, who sees this as yet another way of gaining the attention he so desires.

Note that it's not necessarily a particular style of clothing that's indicative of character type. Dress up each of the basic types in identical garments, such as a uniform, and because of their different predominant roots their appearances will provide quite a contrast. As the Visuddhi-Magga's description makes clear, monks of the three basic character types will wear the same saffron robes in three very different ways.

The kind of jewellery a person chooses can also provide clues as to their character type. If a woman has a strong craving root, she will tend to wear large and flamboyant rings, necklaces and bracelets, and lots of them. If hatred is more dominant within her mental make-up, the kind of jewellery she prefers will be very small and unobtrusive, and the amount she wears will be minimal.

The same principle applies to men – cravers love wearing gold chains, medallions, St Christophers, large rings. They'll also go in for flashy hi-tech multi-functional watches, as much for adornment as for any practical purpose. All a hate type wants from a watch is the correct time; as for jewellery, in his case it's non-existent.

In the area of cosmetics, a craver is often prepared to spend a lot on high-quality make-up in fashionable shades; and her application of lipstick and eye-pencil will show both patience and skill. The hate type may prefer what she regards as a natural look, shunning cosmetics, manicures and perms altogether.

But as mentioned earlier, this form of analysis, although it can be simple, should not be used simplistically. To arrive at an accurate assessment, it's essential to observe a person's behaviour in many different areas over a period of time. The more experience you have of the system, the more attuned you'll become to the intricacies involved.

On the subject of clothes, for example, you need to take note of current styles. Whilst it's true that as a rule hate types wear their clothes tight, there are times when everyone is buying the kind of jeans where you have to lie down on the floor to get your money out of the pockets. Whilst it's equally true that a confused type will go round with clothes baggy and loose, chin unshaven, there are times when that kind of look is fashionable. So a person presenting a dishevelled appearance may well be a craver: it's cravers, after all, who follow the dictates of fashion.

Fashion styles can of course serve as indicators of mental attitudes in a wider context. Forty years ago it was the norm for a man to wear a suit, a clean white shirt and a short-back-and-sides; anything more flamboyant might cause too much of a stir. In recent years, however, it's become more socially acceptable for men openly to express the craving side of their nature. Just as there have been ages when wigs, powder and satin were quite permissible for men, if not *de rigueur*, so in the last few decades there have been times when it has been common for men to have perms or wear pony-tails.

Remember that the question of appearance is only one aspect by which somebody's character can be assessed. Take, for example, the kind of person who walks out of their bedroom in the morning dressed immaculately – clothes stylish, well-matched, clean and pressed; typical of a craver. But have a look inside the room they've left behind – bed unmade, drawers left open and overflowing with clothes, the floor littered with papers, magazines and used coffee mugs. Whilst there's craving in the area of dress, you'd be justified in deciding that there's also evidence of confusion in the character.

On the other hand, someone may assess the quantity of clothes they own and how often they go out shopping and come to the conclusion that they're really not extravagant in that area so they can't be a craver. Maybe not – in the area of dress. But perhaps they hoard furniture, ornaments, records, magazines, potplants . . .

There's a lot of information you can and should gather if your assessments are going to be accurate, but you'll find that weighing up the strengths of the different roots in a particular individual is something that becomes easier and easier as your experience of the system increases.

5

MANNER OF POSTURE

The stance of one of craving temperament is confident and graceful. When he is walking in his usual manner, he walks carefully, puts his foot down slowly, puts it down evenly, lifts it up evenly, and his step is springy.
The stance of one of hating temperament is rigid. He walks as though he were digging with his heels, puts his foot down quickly, lifts it up quickly, and his step is dragged along.
The stance of one of confused temperament is muddled. He walks with a perplexed gait, puts his foot down hesitantly, lifts it up hesitantly, and his step is pressed down suddenly –
Visuddhi-Magga

Bearing in mind that to portray the essence of a particular character type is inevitably to present something of a caricature, we now turn our attention to the way the different types hold themselves, the way they move around.

Cravers, as always, are elegant. Their posture is usually easy, relaxed, yet upright; their stance indicates their confidence, that they're quite at home in their bodies. When they move, they walk smoothly, evenly, fluidly, with an obvious sense of balance. They rarely make much of a noise.

When it comes to sitting, if you watch a group of people enter a room furnished with a variety of chairs, it's invariably the cravers who'll sit down first. In their concern for sensual comfort, they can be very quick to calculate which chair is the softest, which nearest to the source of heat, and promptly make a beeline for it. They're not about to be forced to take a hard-backed chair in a draught because they took too long to make up their minds.

Hate types present a very different picture. They hold themselves rather stiffly, even rigidly. They often seem ill-at-ease, as if they're trying to disappear into the background, and there's a general air of tension about them. You may find a hate type sitting right on the edge of his seat – or sometimes, in his attempt to keep a low profile, leaning so far back in the chair he looks as if he's about to tip over.

When hate types walk around, they move in a stiff and rather jerky fashion. Their feet usually meet the ground with some impact so you're likely to hear them coming. Regardless of the predominant root, one of the most noticeable things about anyone in a bad mood – in other words with hatred present at that particular time – is that they put their feet down with force; floorboards can shake when such a person walks across a room.

The hate type's bottled-up tension will also show in the speed with which he or she rushes impatiently about, the amount of noise they make as they fling open cupboards and bang shut doors. Hate types habitually use more force than is necessary, whatever it is they're doing; the way they turn off a tap or screw up a jam-jar can mean you virtually need to use a wrench to undo it.

Turning to **confused types**, their posture can probably be best described as shambling; they tend to sit slumped, their limbs sprawling in an undisciplined fashion. Indecisiveness being one of the major characteristics of this particular type, their movements can often be hesitant, unsteady, uneven. If you watch a confused type walking along a pavement, there'll be times when his sense of direction seems to waver and he zigzags crab-fashion from side to side. If there's a confused type in a busy shopping mall, he's likely to keep bumping into people, being uncertain how to make his way through the jostling crowds. If you come across someone with one foot poised momentarily in the air, unable to make the decision as to whether or not to put it down, you've come across a confused type.

Confusion can often strike in a panic situation. Many people have had the experience of having so much to do that for a moment they've found themselves frozen motionless.

Perhaps you're giving a party: rushing round buying food and drink, making phone calls, organising the music, moving the furniture . . . The time gets closer and closer for the arrival of the guests and still there's a hundred things to do. Suddenly you find yourself standing in the middle of the kitchen floor, glued to the spot. You don't know which way to turn, what to do next; your mind seems to have switched off. Such a state of indecision is a hallmark of confusion.

6

MANNER OF EATING

*One of **craving temperament** likes eating rich sweet food. When eating, he makes a round lump not too big and eats unhurriedly, savouring the various tastes. He enjoys getting something good. One of **hating temperament** likes eating rough sour food. When eating, he makes a lump that fills his mouth, and he eats hurriedly without savouring the taste. He is aggrieved when he gets something not good. One of **confused temperament** has no settled choice. When eating, he makes a small unrounded lump, and as he eats he drops bits into his dish, smearing his face, with his mind astray, thinking of this and that – Visuddhi-Magga*

People's attitude to food is of course one of the main conditioning factors in determining their body shape. **Cravers** like their food, particularly when it's rich, sweet and succulent, and thus it will come as no surprise to find that they often tend to be overweight. As a rule of thumb, when it comes to body shape, craving males are well-built (and often hirsute), females curvaceous. Hate types of either sex are generally thin, wiry, physically undeveloped. A hate type of forty or fifty may well have the same straight-up-and-down shape they had as a child.

If cravers go out for a meal and food's an area where their craving root is particularly strong, they'll choose rich and intricate dishes, perhaps with unusual or exotic ingredients. For some cravers, quantity is all that matters, but there are also those with a more adventurous bent who are always eager to try out unfamiliar foreign cuisine and would prefer to patronise a new Oriental or Middle-Eastern restaurant rather than the local steak-house.

Many a craver is a gourmet, a connoisseur of fine food. If you're invited to a friend's for dinner and your host is a craver, you're pretty well guaranteed a good meal, attractively presented. Food can be a source of pleasure not only through the senses of smell, taste and touch (in terms of its texture) but also through the sense of sight, and a craver is essentially a person who is concerned with the attainment of pleasure through any or all of the senses.

Cravers with an interest in food will enjoy poring over cookery books, especially those illustrated with colour photographs of lavish dishes. They also like to talk about food (especially if they're on a diet) – two cravers can have a lengthy conversation about the respective merits of different types of chocolate bars. When it comes to cooking, they probably won't stick to the recipes: they operate under the assumption that more equals better, that additions must stand for improvement. Another ounce or so of butter smeared on the chicken, sultanas and sunflower seeds tossed into the salad, slices of fruit or grated chocolate on the pudding, elaborate garnishes of all kinds: these are the marks of the craver.

Unless we're talking about the kind of out-and-out craving where people just tear into their food and binge, cravers eat slowly, savouring the various tastes and appreciating the different textures. And whether they're eating with their hands (as is common practice in some of the Oriental countries) or using a knife and fork, their manners will generally be good. They won't offend their companions' sensibilities by the way they eat – no slurping, chomping or gulping sounds.

Food's not particularly important to **hate types** – they tend to shovel it in so that it goes straight down without touching the sides. For them food is simply fuel – why would anyone want to spend a lot of time and money going out for a gourmet meal? Hate types aren't often concerned about subtleties of taste or texture – given the option, they'd rather have a burger or a TV dinner than haute cuisine. Convenience foods could have been invented with hate types in mind – to spend hours preparing and arranging food is, in their opinion, a waste of time, sheer indulgence. Neither are they particularly interested in displaying decent table manners – for this particular character type, the major concern is speed.

If hate types do have a preference, it's for plain and savoury dishes. If they get given something they don't particularly like, they can be quite upset about it, more so than you'd think the food warranted (anger, as we'll see later, is one of the habitual mental responses of the hate type). They're not keen on sugar in their food or drinks; it's cravers who go for three teaspoons of sugar in their coffee.

Sugarless drinks and minimal consumption of sweets and puddings, however, do not necessarily indicate a hate type. In many cravers, the desire for a fashionable figure is greater than the desire for food. Whilst their bodies may be as slender as a hate type's, it's only because their craving for an impressive appearance is strong enough to keep their appetites in check.

Where cravers are generally orientated towards the physical senses, hate types are more inclined towards things of the mind; they're often idealists. Accordingly, if they should show any interest in the content of their diet, it's likely to be a philosophically-based one – particularly if they come across a philosophy which encourages them in their tendency towards asceticism and giving things up. They may become vegetarians or vegans in accordance with their beliefs about factory farming or animal rights. They may choose a diet like macrobiotics, more concerned about balancing the principles of yin and yang in their meals than in deriving sensual pleasure from them.

As for **the confused type** of personality, if such an individual goes out for a meal and is presented with a multi-course à la carte menu, it can cause him great concern – unless he has a decisive companion whose choices he can quietly copy. Where cravers opt for rich sweet food and hate types prefer plain and savoury, confused types don't really know what they like. If they're asked whether they want to drink tea or coffee, their reply will be along the lines of 'Whichever's easiest' or 'I'll have what you're having.'

When they eat they pile the food on to their fork or spoon in such a manner that some of it at least is bound to fall off. They often find it difficult to keep their minds on what they're doing and while they're eating their attention can wander off anywhere. Accordingly, after they've finished, there may well be crumbs on the table around their plates or on the floor, as well as marks of spillage on their clothes. Jam on the fingers and ketchup-smears round the mouth are similarly indications that confusion is about.

7

MANNER OF SLEEPING

*One of **craving temperament** spreads his bed unhurriedly, lies down slowly, composing his limbs, and he sleeps in a confident manner. When woken, instead of getting up quickly, he gives his answer slowly as though doubtful.*
*One of **hating temperament** spreads his bed hastily anyhow; with his body flung down he sleeps with a scowl. When woken, he gets up quickly and answers as though annoyed.*
*One of **confused temperament** spreads his bed all awry and sleeps mostly face downwards with his body sprawling. When woken, he gets up slowly, saying 'Hum' – Visuddhi-Magga*

A considerable proportion of human existence is spent in sleep, and as the Visuddhi-Magga indicates, there are three quite distinct approaches to the subject.

Cravers are typically relaxed about it; they take their time. Getting into bed at night, they settle their limbs into a comfortable position, lie there quiet and still and just drift off into unconsciousness. Should you need to wake such a person in the middle of the night, he or she will again take their time: wake up slowly, answer you slowly, slowly climb out of bed. When they make their bed in the morning, they'll make sure that they've smoothed out any wrinkles down the bottom, that the sheets and blankets are tucked in all round and the pillows plumped up.

Hate types, on the other hand, are likely to get rather impatient with a craver's lack of urgency and speed. They'll probably consider it quite unnecessary to take time out to smooth the sheets and blankets when bed-making – after all, beds are for being unconscious on, so why bother with such niceties? Their beds may appear neat and tidy when they're made but their orderliness smacks of military precision, compared with the more natural orderliness of a craver's. Sometimes hate types tuck the sheets and blankets in so tightly that the bed's nearly impossible to get into.

At the end of the day, hate types tend to throw themselves down, aiming to get off to sleep as fast as they can. Frowns or scowls are common expressions on the faces of sleeping hate types; they may also grind their teeth. However, their habitually high level of tension can often prove quite an obstacle to the quick descent into unconsciousness they so desire. The degree of physical tension under which it's possible to sleep is nevertheless surprisingly high. Not that such sleep will prove particularly refreshing: it's broken, shallow, restless, jumbled with dreams.

Cravers, dedicated as they are to extracting the maximum of pleasure from any situation, have the better idea when it comes to getting a good night's rest: they have a natural inclination to relax the body out as they lie in bed. Their attitude, though, is no more efficient – a craver's tendency to grasp at pleasant feelings is in the long run just as productive of suffering as is the hate type's impatience.

To wake a hate type up in the middle of the night might not be such a good idea. He or she is likely to answer you rather angrily and jump straight out of bed.

As for **confused types**, they may not quite get round to making their beds, and if they do, their handiwork is unlikely to impress. Wrinkles under the bedcover are not in their case the result of impatient haste but rather evidence of the problems they have keeping their minds on the job of bed-making.

Even when they're asleep confused people can present a rather muddled appearance: the blankets are generally half off, legs or arms hanging out over the sides; often they sleep on their stomachs. And to wake such individuals may prove difficult. It's as though they're hovering in some no man's land between consciousness and unconsciousness and it can feel as though you're just not getting through at all. There's a long delay, then perhaps some sort of mumble – and they'll probably turn over and go straight back to sleep. Confused types like to cling to the warmth and security of their beds, to that happy state where they can be free of all the decision-making and anxiety they're faced with in the waking world.

Note that the fact that someone never makes their bed in the morning, for example, can't on its own be used as concrete evidence of confusion. Cravers might not make their beds through laziness – they'd rather use the time to have a relaxed breakfast before heading off to the office. Hate types might be motivated by impatience – they've got a packed day ahead and they're raring to get on with it; and after all, they'd only have to unmake them again when they get back in at night. Similarly, cravers may lie in bed just as long as confused types, basking in the pleasure of physical relaxation.

The importance of discerning the psychological motivation behind particular traits of behaviour, as we'll see later, makes of character analysis a subtler and more complex business than might at first sight be assumed.

8

MANNER OF WORKING

In the act of sweeping, one of **craving temperament** *grasps the broom well, and he sweeps cleanly and evenly without hurrying or scattering the sand, as if he were strewing flowers. As with sweeping, so too with any action such as washing and dyeing robes and so on: one of craving temperament acts skilfully, gently, evenly and carefully.*

One of **hating temperament** *grasps the broom tightly, and he sweeps uncleanly and unevenly with a harsh noise, hurriedly throwing up the sand on each side. He acts tensely, stiffly and unevenly.*

One of **confused temperament** *grasps the broom loosely, and he sweeps neither cleanly nor evenly, mixing the sand up and turning it over. He acts unskilfully as if muddled, unevenly and indecisively*
– Visuddhi-Magga

Many of the monasteries in the East have extensive sandy or earthen areas in their grounds which are usually swept by the monks at least once a day. Hence in such a monastic setting, the way a man wields his broom can prove a particularly useful pointer as to character type. In the West, sweeping may not be a primary activity but everyone is involved in work of one kind or another. By observing how an individual handles a job of work we can draw some useful conclusions.

What distinguishes **the craver's** approach to a task? Cravers work in a smooth, methodical, relaxed and efficient manner, keeping their attention on what they're doing, not usually allowing their minds to stray off the job in hand. While they're reasonably conscientious in their application, they pace themselves in a way calculated to minimise their own stress levels, and they feel little sense of pressure that there are still more jobs to be done. A craving-type monk won't kick up clouds of dust as he sweeps and he'll leave the monastery grounds smooth and even. A craver involved in any occupation tends to produce work of consistently good quality, work with a certain amount of flair to it.

Generally, cravers do a good job of work, they know it – and they make sure everyone else knows it as well. However, as cravers do tend to be lazy, there are times when they're not averse to doing the minimum they can get away with – as long as they can claim maximum kudos. Cravers are often to be found in high-profile jobs; they're the advertising executives, the sales or managing directors, the chiefs rather than the indians. Expense-account lunches are an indispensable part of their routine and their favourite place for striking deals is the golf-course.

Hate types, on the other hand, may be just as competent as their craving colleagues and get rather more work done besides, but because they don't relate terribly well to the people they work with or the customers they deal with they tend to remain in the background, stuck several rungs down the ladder. They work behind the scenes, often conscientiously but usually missing out on the credit. They may be rather scathing of their craver bosses, and despite their own lower rating in the hierarchy, consider themselves superior.

When it comes to individual tasks, the hate type's style of working is just as distinctive as the craver's. The end-result may well be as good – a clean, neat, tidy job of work – but the means by which he achieves it differ considerably. Hate types usually work quickly, impatiently, vigorously, often rather noisily. They tend to be one-pointed in their approach, not seeing anything but the task in hand.

They'd rather not have to stop to make conversation with somebody passing by nor break off for a cup of tea. And if they do have to, they don't enjoy it – it makes them feel uncomfortable, that they should really be getting on with the job. They want to get all their work finished and out of the way as fast as they can because only then do they feel they can relax. What they fail to appreciate, of course, is that work is an inevitable part of the human condition, and the more tasks they complete, the more they'll find to do. They don't understand that their ideal of a work-free state is simply a myth.

How people respond to interruptions to a particular job they're involved in can be a useful indicator as to how they feel about the job in question. If there's a task that you don't really want to do and someone interrupts you in the middle of it, you'll find you're likely to get somewhat irritable. If on the other hand you're really enjoying what you're doing, you don't mind being interrupted at all. In short, when there's hatred in the mind and you are interrupted, that hatred can mushroom quite rapidly.

Depending on the task in question, the harsh energetic style of the hate type may sometimes mean that whilst the job itself is done well, there's a certain amount of damage left *around* the work area. If he's cleaning a room, he'll hoover the carpet so that it's spotless – but his impatience to get the job over with might mean the hoover's been banged into the skirting-board and the paintwork's looking pretty chipped.

And though the room will be quite free of dust and grime, the furniture and ornaments are just shoved back more or less in the place they were found. Generally speaking, it doesn't occur to hate types to arrange things so that they're pleasing to the eye. Or if it does, they'd probably consider it a waste of time. Anyhow, they're already on to the next job.

A clean, neat, tidy job of work is *not* **the confused type's** forte. Often he only has half his mind on what he's doing and in consequence he works in fits and starts, backtracking on himself or missing bits out altogether.

If a confused type is cooking a meal, he'll get out a couple of onions, peel them, start chopping – then decide that he really ought to get the pudding in the oven first. So he leaves the onions half-chopped and sets to work on cutting up apples – probably without washing the chopping board; a confused type would be unlikely to notice if the apple pie tasted of onion. He may make it through to the end of the pie, only to remember he's forgotten to defrost the meat for the casserole.

At the end of a task a confused type may think he's finished but an impartial observer will have a different view. If he's been cooking a meal, there'll be dirty plates, pots and pans scattered over the worktops and the hob will be spattered with stains where the pans boiled over because he forgot to turn them down. If he's been cleaning a room, sometimes it's done so badly that someone else has to do it all over again – it would have been better if he'd never started. A layer of dust over every surface has the virtue at least of consistency – if a confused type comes along, flicks a duster here and there and wanders off again, you're left with big cleaned streaks surrounded by dust, which can look worse than it did before.

In keeping with their indecisive nature, confused types like to have lots of jobs on the go at once and they're not too concerned about finishing any of them. For example, it was the custom of a particular romantic novelist to keep several typewriters in different rooms in her house, each loaded with a different work in progress. She would move from one half-written manuscript to another as the fancy took her. Over the years, she did in fact get a lot of books published, but the inconsistencies in the plots and even in the names of the characters make them very confusing reading.

9

MANNER OF LOOKING AT OBJECTS

*When one of **craving temperament** sees even a slightly pleasing
visible object, he looks long as if surprised, he seizes on trivial
virtues, discounts genuine faults, and when departing, he does so
with regret as if unwilling to leave.*
*When one of **hating temperament** sees even a slightly unpleasing
visible object, he avoids looking long as if he were tired, he picks out
trivial faults, discounts genuine virtues, and when departing, he
does so without regret as if anxious to leave.*
*When one of **confused temperament** sees any sort of visible object,
he copies what others do: if he hears others criticising, he criticises; if
he hears others praising, he praises: but actually he feels equanimity
in himself – the equanimity of unknowing.*
So too with sounds, and so on – Visuddhi-Magga

An ideal situation to distinguish the ways in which the
different character types respond to visual objects is watching
how a group of people react when a batch of holiday
photographs is handed round.

The cravers will take their time over the pictures, handling each one gently and with care. They will really seem to appreciate the photographer's skill (whether it exists or not), and will make much of whatever there is to make much of: artistry, composition, colour, scenery. Their comments may run along the lines of 'This one of the Chrysler Building's excellent – it really says New York to me', or 'Your sister's very photogenic.' They won't mention that the Chrysler Building's leaning like the Tower of Pisa or that your sister seems to have lost the top of her head.

When they look at an object, cravers see only the good points – they dismiss the faults, however genuine. 'I didn't quite get the focus sharp enough in that one,' the photographer may say. 'But it's such a good composition,' a craver will reply, 'you'd scarcely notice.'

Always attuned to the potential pleasures to be gained, cravers will savour each picture as if they had all the time in the world. **Hate types**, on the other hand, will generally give each little more than a cursory glance, racing through them in a rather uninterested manner and rapidly passing them on to the next person in the group. If that person's a craver, there may by now be a whole pile building up beside them awaiting inspection, whilst their hate-type neighbour sits empty-handed and restlessly twiddling his thumbs.

Hate types probably won't have a lot to say about the photographs; what they do say will more often than not be critical. 'Where did you get these developed? The colours are pretty unnatural.' Or, 'I like the way you've got the telegraph pole growing out of his head!'

And **confused types**? They'll probably keep quiet at first – until they hear an opinion they can copy. If someone says, 'I think this one's excellent', they'll agree. If someone else comments, in reference to the same picture, 'That was a waste of a shot!', they'll also agree. Confused types tend not to have their own opinions – they look for cues from other people, because for themselves, they just don't know. And if at the end of the day some of the photographs are smudged with greasy thumbmarks, there's a fair chance that there was at least one confused type in the group.

If a craver's out driving, he'll somehow manage to see everything at once: the road in front, the countryside on either side, the woman leaning out of a cottage window, the cat stuck up a tree. His eyes seem to be on antennae, constantly scanning the environment for fresh stimuli to provide fresh pleasure. Hate types, when driving, will look at nothing but the road. They just don't notice the countryside, however beautiful; the woman could fall out of her cottage window as they drove past and they'd never know. Her fall might also escape the notice of a confused-type driver – not because he's concentrating on the road, more likely because he's sunk in daydreams or worrying about being lost.

The craving, hating and confused responses to objects of sight also occur in relation to objects of the other senses – hearing, smelling, tasting, touching. Listen to the comments made after a concert. Do people say 'I've never heard that piece played so well!' – or, 'Pity the violinist couldn't keep up with the rest' – or, 'What did *you* think?'

Data can also be gathered by listening to the sort of remarks people make about a meal, a walk or a book. If they tend to be positive – perhaps over-positive, that's evidence of the craving root. If they're negative – perhaps over-negative, there's certainly some degree of hatred in the character. And those who just cannot be pinned down one way or the other, who seem to have no views of their own – they are the confused.

10

OTHER EXTERNAL SIGNS

Apart from the six areas specifically mentioned in the Visuddhi-Magga (manner of dress, posture, eating, sleeping, working and looking at objects) the general principles behind the craving/hating/confused approaches can be seen to operate in just about any field of life you care to consider.

How, for example, do the different character types handle their money? Cravers like to spend – they love doing business by credit card and their bank accounts are often in the red. Cravers with flourishing overdrafts have been known to go into town insisting that they're just going to look – they're certainly not going to buy anything. They return with perhaps a roll of curtain material, a pair of shoes, a kitchen gadget – sales bargains that they just couldn't resist.

Hate types, on the other hand, will often come back from the shops empty-handed, even when they really do need something. They've always got a few pounds in their pockets and they dislike being overdrawn; they prefer to make do with what they've got and remain unencumbered by debts.

Handwriting can also provide some useful clues: a craver's is generally large, bold, fluent, perhaps embellished with loops and flourishes and liberally sprinkled with exclamation marks. Cravers may choose to use red or green ink or flashy personalised stationery.

A hate type's writing is likely to be neat and small – sometimes very small; it will probably be angular rather than rounded. Given their penchant for excessive force, hate types often press their pens down very hard, with the result that what they've written on the top sheet of a pad can often be clearly read several pages on.

And if the writing in a letter slopes backwards and forwards and meanders its way over the page, shunning straight lines, there's a good chance the writer was confused. Crumples in the paper, coffee stains on the envelope and stamps at an unusual angle provide additional evidence of confusion.

Of course, someone whose handwriting shows evidence of confusion may display craving, for example, in their attitude to clothes or food. It's also important to recognise that even within the same area of activity different roots can operate in different strengths at different times.

For many people, early morning is a time when confusion manifests strongly; later on in the day the predominant root may be craving or intelligence or faith. Many women have observed the relationship between states of mind and the menstrual cycle. At ovulation, sensual-desire – the root of craving – tends to predominate; pre-period they commonly experience a dullness and unwieldiness of mind, symptomatic of confusion, sometimes accompanied by irritability or depression, which derive from the root of hatred.

Similarly, there are those who find that their mental states are affected by the full moon – at that particular point in the

lunar cycle confusion may be the root they note most frequently. Statistics concerning road accidents bear this out:
there are noticeably more round about full-moon time, when
drivers under the influence of confusion take risks that at other
times they'd be very wary of.

As none of us is separate from our environment, we can tell
a lot about people by observing the environment they create.
How does each character type approach their external surroundings? Whether they live in mansions, bedsits or car-
avans, cravers ideally like to keep their homes neat, clean and
well decorated. In fact it can seem that they're forever
decorating, whether by way of wallpaper and paint or by way
of ornaments, pictures, potplants, flowers. They may buy a
piece of furniture and be absolutely enamoured of it at the
time, find after a week or so that it's not quite right after all and
end up consigning it to the lumber room. Their home presents
a picture which is constantly changing.

Cravers like to arrange their rooms in such a fashion that
when they look around a sense of pleasure and well-being
springs up within them. A vase of flowers or a group of
ornaments will be positioned with care – an inch or so too close
or too far apart and the balance and artistry are destroyed, the
visual pleasure lost. Comfort is also a primary concern for the
craver: witness the large cushioned armchairs and the radia-
tors turned up high or the fire blazing in the grate.

A hate type's home may be just as neat and clean as the
craver's, but it can be somehow a little too tidy, a little too
empty, even austere. It may well be very functional and easily
managed, but it tends to be rather a sterile place, lacking in life,
colour and warmth. The rooms are devoid of that personal
touch which comes so naturally to the craver – they might just
as well be rooms in a hotel. Decorations in the form of posters,
pictures, ornaments, flowers are rare if not absent altogether.

Hate types dislike clutter and incline towards sparseness
and space – a Japanese-like arrangement of three twigs would

be more up their street than vases overflowing with a
profusion of flowers and greenery – if indeed they could be
bothered with any kind of decoration. There are of course
times when a spartan approach to decor represents the height
of current fashion and then trend-setting cravers are keen to
adopt minimalist tastes.

In the case of confused types, their homes are a jumble, bits
and pieces everywhere: clothes dropped behind settees and
chairs, used mugs and plates on tables and carpets, papers,
magazines, crumbs and dust scattered over every available
surface. Drawers and doors are often not quite closed – and if a
cupboard does happen to be shut, anyone opening it would be
wise to stand well back if they want to avoid an avalanche of
clutter.

The same themes can be seen to continue on into the
garden. Not everybody's interested in the soil – even if they
are, cravers may be too lazy to bother and would rather
employ a gardener. Their ideal garden is colourful, alive and
again, beautifully arranged. In practice, it may be rather
overcrowded – working as always on the principle that more is
better, they find it very difficult to leave a garden-centre
without some kind of purchase. Their favourite plants have
bold luscious leaves and big flowers; they tend to opt for rather
exotic specimens, regardless of the fact they're unlikely to
make it through an English winter.

Cravers' gardens, like their homes, are designed to give
pleasure. Ideally they're inviting places and productive of
many forms of sensual delight – they're visually pleasing,
fragrant and filled with birdsong or the ripple of running
water.

Many people go for the wild overgrown look in gardens so
a confused type's might be more popular than he'd expect.
Even the bindweed can present an attractive sight, so long as
it's not strangling too many of the surrounding shrubs. But
watch out for the fork and trowel left rusting in the soil when

he forgot to put them away, or the empty Coke cans buried in the long grass of the lawn.

Hate-type gardeners would rather grow inconspicuous alpines than a craver's camellias or peonies. Their beds and borders are laid out with military precision and woe betide any weed that tries to infiltrate them. There are often fair quantities of bare tilled soil to be seen between the plants – in contrast with a craver's garden, where every square inch is filled. If they're horticulturally inclined, hate types like to identify their plants by the correct botanical titles. Where the craver may refer to smoke bush and love-in-the-mist, the hate type prefers to speak of *cotinus coggygria* and *nigella*.

As always, their approach inclines towards efficiency rather than aesthetics. Hate types who find themselves lumbered with gardens that they never really wanted might well approve of the man who suggested concreting over the flower-beds and replacing the lawn with plastic grass so the only gardening involved was hosing it all down.

STATES OF MIND

Having described the external signs, the Visuddhi-Magga then goes on to describe what it calls 'states occurring'. These states are the typical attitudes and habitual mental responses associated with the different roots. And whereas the external clues generally speaking can be seen to fall into three simple and basic categories, when we turn to states of mind we need to consider all six of the roots of character.

Although as we've seen each pair of roots shares the same basic thrust – towards an object for craving and faith, away from it for hatred and intelligence, immobile with indecision in the case of confusion and speculation – each of the six produces a different and quite distinctive set of habitual mental states. The negative roots – craving, hatred, confusion – expressed in inefficient mental states inevitably lead to suffering; the positive roots – faith, intelligence, speculation – support the growth of efficient states, which lead to happiness in the world.

Making inferences about the kind of mental actions an individual is currently performing can be rather a tricky business. There are many experienced actors amongst us – many of us, for example, are very skilled at concealing our emotions. Some people take this skill to its limits, pushing down with such speed all evidence of unwanted mental behaviour (things like anger, envy, jealousy) that the individuals themselves have no idea that any inefficiency has arisen.

To claim the ability to know what kind of states occur in another person's mind may be regarded as presumptuous. Nevertheless, leaving aside the question of telepathic abilities, there's a potential store-house of information available to the careful and unbiased observer – facial expressions and body-language, for example, the words people use, or the words they significantly omit. Given the interdependence of mind and body, our mental actions and attitudes will inevitably manifest to some degree in our physical responses. It's extraordinarily easy, for example, for someone to give away the secrets of their state of mind through the tone of their voice.

Everybody knows at some level when someone's mind is full of hatred or craving. People just don't want to be around an individual who's radiating dislike of others with every movement and every word. Craving can have a similarly daunting effect. Take the kind of person who craves for attention, who at every opportunity turns the conversation back to himself – given the choice, most will steer well clear of such an individual.

Again, it's necessary to be wary of over-simplification: the same person may show signs of craving on one occasion, intelligence on another, speculation on yet another. What's important is to get a general, balanced overview of a personality – and that, as we've said, takes time.

11

States of Mind: THE CRAVING TYPE

*In one of **craving temperament** there is frequent occurrence of such states as deceit, fraud, pride, evilness of wishes, greatness of wishes, discontent, foppery and personal vanity – Visuddhi-Magga*

The most important thing in life to cravers is pleasure – the more the better. Whatever they regard as a source of pleasure they'll try to acquire. They like to have more possessions, more friends, more parties, more clothes, bigger meals, stronger stimulation, higher status, more leisure-time. Most of their actions are geared towards attaining pleasurable ends; many of their decisions in life are taken with the most pleasurable option in mind.

In the search for constant sensory stimulation, cravers often like to have lots of possible channels open to them. They'll have the television on while they're doing the housework and the idea of a car without a radio and tape-player would horrify them. A craver might put a record on in one room, wander into the next room and put the television on, go into the kitchen to fix themselves a sandwich, then pick up the phone to call a friend.

Cravers never want to miss anything; they always like to know what's going on. After all, they might lose out on a pleasurable experience.

To ensure ready access to pleasant feelings, cravers are often collectors. Whatever they discover gives them pleasure – books, videos, motorbikes, model aircraft, pottery, paintings, friends – they surround themselves with, aiming thereby to have a source of happiness constantly on tap. If one particular book or film doesn't satisfy them, they can sift through their collection till they find the one that does.

Cravers are by no means always aware that they're steering their lives in accordance with their cravings. Rather than acknowledge what's really going on in their minds, they'll come up with all sorts of superficially commendable reasons for acquiring or hanging on to an object of desire. They tend to rationalise their cravings away, sometimes conning themselves and indeed other people as to their true motivation. 'I feel I really had to get a CD player,' a craver might say. 'CDs last much longer than records so it's obviously a good investment.' Or, 'It's so cold at the moment I must be burning up calories at a rate of knots – I'd better have a chocolate bar.'

One woman, making a hasty assessment of her own character, came to the erroneous conclusion that she was a hate type. Therefore, she decided, it was only sensible to spend a lot of money on clothes – after all, it would help to balance her character out a bit. In fact, in the matter of appearance if nothing else, she was most definitely a craver. By filling up a wardrobe of cavernous proportions she was simply indulging her tendency to crave, whether she was prepared to acknowledge it or not.

Things 'just happen' to cravers. A man 'just happens' to pass by the house of a woman he's interested in at the moment she's walking out of her gate. Or perhaps he 'just happens' to be having a coffee in the café where she goes for lunch. He may honestly believe it's a complete coincidence, oblivious of the fact that such situations are often engineered as a direct result of his craving.

Cravers are not averse to misleading themselves, they're not averse to misleading other people. And as long as they get what they want, they're not always overly concerned about how they go about getting it – whether the means they choose are legitimate, semi-legitimate or downright illegal.

They may not always go so far as to break a rule but they're often rather skilled at bending them – again, perhaps not even realising that they're doing it. A child, for example, was offered the choice of one item out of a collection of toys. After some deliberation, she got hold of a doll, mounted it on a donkey, made off with her 'one item' and was quite bemused when she was told she'd done something wrong. Craving is by no means the prerogative of adults.

In a place like a meditation centre there are often rules which restrict eating to mealtimes and forbid talking altogether. Unsurprisingly, those rules are not always upheld and those who break them are invariably the cravers in the group. If there's a room with apple cores on the ground beneath the window and chocolate wrappers in the waste-bin, the occupant is a craver. 'I can see it might get chaotic if everyone started talking,' a craver may reason when he's bursting to communicate with someone, 'but surely the rule isn't meant to apply *all* the time.' So he has a quick whisper, quite unaware of the craving that motivates him.

In the Buddha's day, there was a group of monks referred to as 'the group of six' who were cravers *par excellence*. Their behaviour forced the Buddha to formulate many new rules and modify existing rules in order to preserve the good name of the Order. It might seem that the life-style of a Buddhist monk, as compared with that of the average Westerner, would leave little room for sensory indulgence; apart from anything else, he is only permitted to own eight possessions. The group of six, however, were highly imaginative when it came to indulging their cravings.

At one time, for example, they took to wearing coloured sandals. This keen interest in fashion was felt to be unbecoming in a monk, and the Buddha made the wearing of such sandals an offence. The group of six were then to be seen sporting ordinary brown sandals but with coloured straps, and so the rule had to be further refined. They bounced right back with a variety of strange and unusual footwear, including 'sandals pointed with rams' horns, sandals ornamented with scorpions' tails, sandals sewn round with peacocks' tail feathers'. Again the Buddha had to make a ruling – and again the group of six found their way round it, wearing 'sandals decorated with lion-skins, with tiger-skins, with otter-skins, with cat-skins, with squirrel-skins, with owl-skins'. The ruling on footwear was tightened further still, and the group of six turned to other avenues to express their craving.

If it gets them what they want, cravers may be prepared to bend the truth, if they don't actually lie. A college student, arriving half-an-hour late for a tutorial, excused himself by saying 'Sorry I'm late – the car was playing up.' He *was* late and the car *was* playing up. While both statements were accurate, he intentionally implied a link which wasn't actually there: he would have been late whether his car had malfunctioned or not.

Cravers can also on occasion be fraudulent. Deceit and fraud, as listed in the Visuddhi-Magga, are in fact opposing faces of the same quality. Deceit looks inwards – you bend the truth, for example, to save yourself trouble; it doesn't necessarily damage anyone else at all. Fraud looks outwards – you deceive other people to get what you want, causing them damage or loss in the process.

There's a story in the Pali Canon about a group of monks who had gone to stay in a town called Vajji when it was hit by famine. Needless to say, almsfood became very difficult to obtain.

According to Buddhist philosophy, giving, whether of food or anything else, is a meritorious action (that is, an efficient action productive of pleasurable resultants). The amount of merit generated depends on factors like the value of the gift and the purity of the motive of the giver. It also depends on how freed from hatred and craving is the mind of the recipient – rather an alien concept to most Westerners.

During the famine, one of the monks came up with the idea of spreading it about that their group contained many who were highly advanced: those skilled in states of deep meditation, those possessed of psychic powers, those who were well on the way to enlightenment, those who had actually attained that goal.

Delighted that monks of such calibre had chosen to visit their town, that they had such a potential source of merit in their midst, the townspeople were as generous as they could be – 'they gave not to parents, they gave not to wife and children, they gave not to slave or servant, they gave not to friend or colleague, they gave not to blood-relations, as they gave to the monks'.

This scheme came to light when the group of monks, along with many others from the same famine-stricken region, went to visit the Buddha. The other monks were 'lean, wretched, of a bad colour, having become very yellow, their veins standing out all over their bodies', whilst the monks from Vajji were 'handsome, of rounded features, their complexions bright, their skins clear'. The Buddha soon worked out what had been going on.

There are people nowadays who see nothing wrong with some minor fiddling on their Tax Return – 'Everybody does it!' – or twisting or withholding facts when making an insurance claim – 'That's what insurance is for!' Smuggling an extra bottle of scotch through Customs is something some people do as a matter of course.

Cravers can be insatiable in their quest for pleasure – this inevitably leads to states of discontent. A new car or a new computer may initially produce lots of pleasant feelings, but as the weeks pass and the novelty wears off, their attention turns to the bigger and better cars and computers that they *haven't* got and their sense of dissatisfaction mounts.

This is a syndrome the advertising industry has turned to its own great profit. Advertisements can encourage people to believe that their lives are incomplete if they haven't modernised their kitchen; that they're nobodies without the right sort of credit card. Advertisers thrive on discontent.

The obsession with pleasure can also mean that cravers are often not punctual: if they're enjoying what they're doing, they find it very difficult to tear themselves away. For example, one woman had to make a train journey every week to attend an evening class; every week she'd find herself rushing to the station and barely making it on to the train. She decided she needed to be more disciplined and so organised her schedule that she even had time to sit and drink a cup of coffee before she left home. She really enjoyed the coffee – so much so that she decided to have another . . . She ended up rushing to the station and barely making it on to the train.

Taking a longer-term view is something at which cravers are not very good. In fact, however astute and quick-witted they appear to be, when it comes to areas where their craving's strong, they're actually pretty stupid. They can't see further than the immediate gratification of their desires, than the pleasure of the moment; it just doesn't occur to them that they'll experience pain in the future as a direct and unavoidable result of their indulgence.

Cravers are reluctant to let go of things, which means they can sometimes find it very hard to say goodbye. One woman who made regular visits to a neighbour found it so difficult to tear herself away that she had to get her husband to ring her up there on the pretext she was wanted at home. Not that she was necessarily always enjoying herself – she just found it impossible to leave. To witness two cravers trying to part from each other can be a discomfiting experience, especially if the observer is a hate type.

A primary source of pleasure for cravers is people. Cravers need people – as an audience, for approval, even for disapproval (anything, so long as they're noticed). They like to be with them, to talk to them, to touch them, to look at them, to quarrel with them, and they can soon feel lonely and insecure unless there are plenty of them passing in and out of their daily round – which is why the family is often so important to cravers.

Parties, pubs, committee meetings, weddings – cravers will take any opportunity to relate. Perhaps one bumps into an acquaintance on the street: 'Can't stop,' he says, 'got to pick my daughter up from school – I'm already ten minutes late.' Ten minutes later still, once he's finished catching up on all the news, he finally dashes off.

As people are their speciality, cravers are often very skilled at relating. They can be charm itself when they want something out of somebody – or quite dismissive if it turns out he hasn't got what they want. They are very good at telling people what they want to hear and might be shocked at the idea that some would consider their skill in flattery to be lying or deception. A craver is not the right person to ask if you want an honest opinion.

One man travelling in Afghanistan wanted to catch a train to his next destination. He asked a local where the railway station was and whether or not trains ran to the place he wanted to get to. The local gave him directions to the station, which he said was about a mile or so up the road, and explained that the trains he wanted stopped there at frequent intervals throughout the day.

The traveller was delighted to hear this and he set off for the station – or at least in the direction he'd been told the station lay. Eventually he discovered the truth: there were no trains going to his destination, neither was there a station nor even railway lines: the railroad had never got to that part of Afghanistan and probably wasn't scheduled to for another hundred years.

Cravers are also prone to exaggeration. One man was unable to attend a friend's party. 'You missed a great evening,' the host later remarked, 'there were crowds of people!' It in fact turned out that the guests had numbered ten. A skilled character analyst will find no problem in interpreting a craver's words – he'll automatically translate 'stunning' or 'brilliant' into 'quite good' and divide any numbers mentioned by a factor of at least three or four.

Generally speaking, what keeps cravers on the straight and narrow is not so much their conscience, not that they feel they'll be letting themselves down if they tell a lie or break the law – what bothers them is that other people might find them out. Desiring above all else to maintain their image, they really dislike the idea that others might not see them as they want to be seen. Some cravers, if they reckon they'll never be caught, would try and get away with murder. It's fear of blame that stops them – their sense of shame is often minimal.

Cravers, on the whole, have a good opinion of themselves – too good, some might say. However modest their words, inside they think they're the greatest. They can be utterly without skills in a particular area yet quite confident they can tackle the job. There are many different ways in which pride can surface: pride of age, pride of youth, pride of race, pride of sex, pride of body, pride of looks, pride of education. Some people think they're better than anybody else because they've got a degree. Others may consider education irrelevant – *they're* the best because they're building themselves a body worthy of Arnold Schwarzenegger.

Pride of looks – personal vanity – is a common characteristic of cravers. Whatever it costs them, such people like to look their best. Regardless of the dangers of skin cancer, they may bask in the blazing sun for hour upon hour in pursuit of a creditable tan. Regardless of possible medical risks – and regardless of expense – they may get their noses remodelled or their faces lifted. If obesity's a problem, they may even consider having their jaws wired up or their stomachs stapled as an acceptable way of curtailing food intake and reducing their bulk to a fashionable size.

Because they're interested in people, cravers are often proud of their friends – the people they know are invariably (so they say) the leading lights in their fields. They may also go in for name-dropping, believing that the fame, power or glory – the special quality – of an acquaintance (however remote) somehow rubs off on them. If someone tells you that their father shook hands with the Dalai Lama's brother or that Benny Hill was their grandfather's milkman, you're pretty safe in chalking him up as a craver. Along similar lines, one woman in Thailand, wanting to learn how to meditate, went and sought out the man who taught meditation to the King; only the man who taught the King could be good enough for her.

The inflated self-esteem of cravers leads them to wish for greatness often far beyond their current capacities. They love to see their names in print – better still, in lights. A part-time artist who'd be lucky to get exhibited in the village hall thinks his works are worthy of the Tate. A shorthand-typist reckons if they made her managing director she'd really sort the company out.

Through greatness of wishes, a man may describe himself as an artist, though no one has ever seen any of his paintings. A clerical worker may consider herself an actress because that's what she would be if only she got the breaks. In keeping with their as yet unrecognised genius, cravers will make sure that whatever equipment they need for their craft is top of the line. If they become interested in photography, they'll buy the most expensive camera they can afford – they assume they're going to be brilliant and therefore nothing but the best will do.

Cravers are often ambitious, they believe they have enormous potential – if only their talents were recognised. And greatness of wishes can be closely allied with discontent – as in the case of the reasonably talented but unsuccessful musician who felt his genius was such that he ought to be supported by society.

If anyone should get in the way of such a person, he may well come to regret it – evilness of wishes, the wish to harm those considered obstacles to his desires, is another characteristic of the craver. Though one who falls foul of a craver in this way should not take it personally: the craver's main concern is not generally the fate of his victim – all he cares about is what he wants. If he's after a promotion, a subtle piece of backstabbing may do a wonderful job in clearing his path of rivals. His intention isn't exactly to do his rival down – he just wants to get the promotion he knows he deserves.

Deceitful, conceited, grasping, vain, malicious – it doesn't add up to a particularly pretty picture. But a craver may possess charm, skill in relating to others and the ability to put people at their ease, such that his presence makes for harmony rather than conflict. And remember: no individual is a pure character type.

12

States of Mind: THE HATE TYPE

*In one of **hating temperament** there is frequent occurrence of such states as anger, enmity, disparaging, domineering, envy and avarice – Visuddhi-Magga*

Just as craving can range from rampant to mild, so does hatred cover a whole spectrum of mental states from anger and resentment, through impatience and irritability, right down to a subtle, almost imperceptible sense of flatness, a feeling that life is somehow lacking in joy and purpose. But however strong or weak the hatred, its motive is the same: it wants to destroy, to reject, to have done with, to do away with. While craving wants more of life, is life-affirming, hatred is life-denying.

Taking the human race as a whole, hate types are actually less common than cravers. In the last analysis, craving is the root fundamental to the human condition – as evidenced by the fact that when brought face to face with death, the majority crave for life to continue, whatever they may have said beforehand. The ones who aren't craving for this particular life to go on might be craving for heaven or an afterlife of some kind. Most people do want to go on – somehow, somewhere. The pure hate type, if such an individual did exist, would prefer to be blotted out – he'd be aiming for the big black hole, the end, annihilation.

Whether as a root of behaviour it's predominant or not, hatred is unquestionably a very real force in many people. Hate types invariably see the bad side of life, that 'Life is hard and then you die'. They're inclined always to tune into the faults, the errors, the imperfections. And whatever situation you put them in, they can always find something to complain about or criticise. Like the woman who, looking round a beautiful house full of valuable antiques, was heard to comment: 'Of course, I wouldn't want that myself – all that dusting!'

One man became very familiar with the critical approach of the hate type when he had a job where he was working alongside a colleague who was always grumbling about the boss. He couldn't control the staff, she said; he couldn't organise his way out of a paper bag; all in all he was the worst employer she'd ever worked for. As the man got to know his colleague better, he came to realise that she could grumble about just about anything. In due course, the boss left and a new one took over. It wasn't long before the woman had him worked out: he couldn't control the staff; he couldn't organise his way out of a paper bag; he was the worst boss she had ever worked for.

If a colleague comes up with a new idea, a hate type will pounce upon it and tear it to bits, taking pains to point out exactly how this new scheme could never work: 'That's all very well but . . .' That's one reason why in a work situation promotions often pass such an individual by – what boss would want to help up the ladder somebody who's never prepared to strike out into new territory, to take the occasional risk?

With their tendency towards cynicism, scepticism and sarcasm, hate types can make excellent critics. Their concern is not so much to provide a balanced, impartial assessment – what they're good at is describing exactly what is *wrong* with the latest novel, play or film. They excel at damning with faint praise and they can be masters of the put-down. A successful but unpopular media personality once asked a journalist who was interviewing him why it was that people always seemed to take an instant dislike to him. 'It saves time,' the journalist replied.

Humour is an area where hatred is often given full rein; there are some comedians who will sharpen their wits against any target. They'll make jokes against women, particularly mothers-in-law and wives; jokes against students, politicians, royalty, pensioners; jokes against the physically or mentally handicapped; jokes against Jews, Poles, the Irish, the English.

The hate type might argue that he's only being realistic, that the faults he's detected are quite genuine. The fact of the matter is that every situation has a positive side and a negative side. The hate type ignores the positive, the craver ignores the negative; both have a view which is unrealistic because both see only a partial picture.

If a craver and a hate type go to the same place on holiday, the craver will return full of how charming the people were, how glorious the sunsets, how magnificent the architecture. Ask the hate type how he got on and you'd be forgiven for thinking he went to a different place – the food was too greasy, the sun too hot, if it wasn't the beggars who were hassling him it was the mosquitoes. He'd much rather have gone somewhere where there weren't any people at all.

Unlike cravers, hate types don't need people; they don't particularly like people. People, with their raw emotions, their loves, their hates, their petty intrigues, their trivial opinions –

they're messy and complicated; they disturb and corrupt the orderliness and harmony of life as the hate type thinks it should be. The world could be a wonderful place – if it wasn't for all those people.

It's not that hate types don't have feelings and emotions themselves – it's rather the case that their feelings are often more intense, more deeply rooted than those of cravers, who typically wear their hearts on their sleeves. And frightened by their own intensity, hate types often keep themselves under strict control; they dislike and distrust the craver's extravagant emotional displays. Because they think that it's people who stir up their passions, they conclude that getting rid of them altogether is the way to allay their own inner turmoil. They try to be free of relationships and the responsibilities they entail, though generally life has a way of catching up with them and presenting them with exactly what they don't want.

If a hate type does find himself faced with a responsibility, he takes it very seriously and will do all he can to discharge it. Cravers, however, may promise the earth but are generally too lazy to be particularly conscientious and will soon be looking for ways to slide out from under their obligations.

When they do come into contact with other members of the human race, hate types don't relate easily. They don't understand people, they don't empathise with them. In a household of cravers, the occupants will always want to know how the others are, what they're doing, where they're going, who they're going with. A group of hate types could live in the same house or flat and if one of them were to die it might be a matter of days before his absence was noticed. Hate types can be very tunnel-visioned in their approach to life – one reason they may seem to lack compassion is that they just don't see what's going on around them.

Hate types can come across as brusque, aloof, cold, even rude. They're often socially inept and not immediately easy to like. George Eliot captured the tone of the hate type when she described a man as having no red blood in his veins; she said that if somebody put a drop of it under a magnifying-glass all they'd see would be semi-colons and parentheses.

Hate types often have a strong streak of perfectionism and can be ruthlessly efficient in putting their plans into action, impatient with and intolerant of the more leisurely pace of craving colleagues. One man particularly disliked having to work in a group – it made him feel threatened because the standards of other people never seemed as high as his own. Along similar lines, consider the librarian whose impressively efficient system is continually being fouled up by the public coming in and taking out the books.

Privacy and personal space are very important to hate types. They firmly discourage people from dropping in on them unannounced and they would prefer it if their houses were surrounded by tall hedges or walls. Taken to extremes, this love of solitude produces the kind of individual who shuts himself away from all association with his fellows, who chooses for his home an isolated moorland cottage or forest cabin. However, you can also find hate types in the city: they appreciate the anonymity that the urban environment provides.

Hate types can be very bossy and domineering. Two women once found themselves washing up teacups together after a public lecture. One was in her mid-forties, sophisticated and successful; she ran a photographic company with her husband and was responsible for employing models, getting the sets together and handling all of the financial side of the business. The other was in her early twenties and had just left college.

'I really don't know what was going on there,' the older woman later reported. 'I found her telling me how full to fill the sink, how to wash the cups up, where to put them . . . I was totally intimidated.' She was a craver – her companion was a hate type.

★　★　★

Perhaps this is the point at which to make a rather sweeping generalisation and say that men tend towards hatred, women towards craving. On the whole, it's women who show their feelings and who spend hour upon hour discussing their friends, relations, colleagues, neighbours. Feelings don't have the same importance for men – they tend to keep their conversation centred around more impersonal issues, like politics, religion, cars or sport.

Considerable research has of course been carried out on the topic of the differences between the sexes. One experiment involved four children: a pair of boys and a pair of girls. The boys, who were strangers to each other, were taken to a room equipped with a selection of toys and then left to play, their behaviour being observed by the researchers through a two-way mirror. The girls, also strangers, were left together in another similar room.

The researchers noticed a clear distinction in the way each pair approached the situation. The boys became engrossed in a train-set; their conversation was concerned with where to put the signal-box, how many carriages to couple together. The girls, on the other hand, showed less interest in the toys – they wanted to know about each other: where they lived, where they went to school, what their parents did, what their friends were like.

Obviously, it's by no means the case that men are invariably hate types and women cravers – everyone will have come across instances of men who dress beautifully, love spending money and relate with ease and of women who care nothing for clothes or make-up and prefer solitude to society. But as a rule of thumb, men are biased towards the hate root, women towards that of craving.

Physical surroundings aren't particularly important to hate types – they tend to live more in the mind, to be orientated towards the intellect rather than sensuality. They dislike the hugs and kisses that are typical of the craver's mode of relating

– though watch out for the hate type who's been involved in encounter or therapy groups and has adopted 'touchy' behaviour as a learned response.

Their bodies are usually kept under considerable tension (perhaps expressed in twitches or the grinding of teeth) and they may well in later life suffer from arthritis or other tension-related diseases. Generally well-disciplined, they don't like to perceive themselves as weak in any way and consider the craver's concern over physical ailments (which can shade into hypochondria) as sheer indulgence.

Idealism is a common characteristic of the hate type and accordingly he takes a strict approach to laws and rules. You would be most unlikely, for example, to find his car parked on double yellow lines. Where a craver will have little hesitation in pulling up directly outside a shop, paying no heed to the inconvenience he causes to other motorists, a hate type will drive on until he finds a legal parking place.

Hate types can get very intense about the issues that concern them, whether it be nuclear arms, immigration or conservation. They may tell you – often in impassioned tones – how a particular piece of green belt should never be desecrated by roads and most certainly not by houses. They will explain – often at length – how such land is part of our national heritage, how vital it is to keep it unspoiled and pristine, free from human tampering.

Their dreams may be commendable but their tunnel-visioned idealism neglects to concern itself with, say, those people who need somewhere to live. The idealism of hate types can often blind them to the very real plight of their fellows. You can also find hate types in the opposing camp: 'These people must be housed at all costs – let's build all over the city parks,' such an individual may say, completely disregarding the benefits the parks provide.

The causes a hate type espouses may be unquestionably noble ones – few would seriously criticise an ideal like world peace – but his passion about them can be generated by hatred. A positive vision of how he thinks things could be will certainly play a part in motivating his actions, but more fundamental is his desire to reject the current state, to destroy the way things actually are. Outbreaks of violence during demonstrations for peace are more common than the pacifist might like to admit.

A hate type may show a vehement dislike of the world of business and commerce; he also tends to put a high value on the concept of purity. If he's a photographer he would probably rather work in black and white than colour, regardless of current photographic trends. If a musician, he may well prefer to use period instruments, the kind that Bach or Mozart had in mind when they originally wrote their pieces.

The hate type's idealistic approach to life can, on the surface, seem quite reasonable. One such individual, on being shown by a craving friend his collection of CDs, commented that in his opinion, music should always be live. Superficially this might sound fair enough (though if anyone gives it any thought they'll soon realise its impracticality) – it was in fact a subtle put-down of his friend's collection, an expression of hatred disguised under an idealistic veneer.

Such an attitude also indicates another of the hate type's characteristics: envy. They're not happy with other people's success; they're often killjoys who delight in taking the wind from others' sails. It's not necessarily that they want what someone else has got (covetousness is the province of cravers) – their concern lies in depriving others of their pleasure.

Think of Scrooge and his 'Bah, humbug!' attitude to Christmas. Nowadays particularly, Christmas is an occasion that could have been tailor-made for cravers: lots of food, lots of drink, lots of entertainment, lots of relating. Today Scrooges still walk the streets, moaning about the crowds in shops, the dross shown on the television, office parties – moaning particularly about the expense.

Hate types tend to be miserly – they don't like to give and they don't like to share, whether it's money, possessions or time. Again, they may disguise their negative tendency with a veil of purist ideals. They may refuse to buy Christmas cards or presents – 'It's too commercialised nowadays.' They may refuse to buy the family a television – 'It's better if the kids learn to make their own entertainment.'

But the keynote, the aim, of hatred is destruction, in whatever degree. It can of course lead to injury, murder, even genocide. As an extreme case, witness Jack the Ripper, whose murders were supposedly motivated by an idealistic desire to rid the world of prostitutes. A couple of millennia earlier, a Roman statesman called Cato developed a passionate desire to raze to the ground the city of Carthage. Whenever he spoke in the Senate – whether about government elections or the price of corn – his speeches always concluded with the same words: 'And Carthage must be destroyed.' It was.

On a less extreme level, the Pali Canon tells of a hate-type monk named Kappitaka who had made his home in a nice quiet cemetery, just the place for getting on with his meditation. Hate types really don't like it when their peace is disturbed, and when a nun died and a group of her fellows gathered round her tomb weeping and wailing, Kappitaka got very angry indeed. In fact he got so angry that he destroyed the tomb and scattered the materials all over the site.

As another more recent example of the hate type's destructiveness: a woman became so incensed by the caterpillars that infested her roses that she took to picking them off the leaves, one by one, and meticulously cutting each of them into pieces.

As well as being prone to outbursts of anger, hate types can make fine long-term enemies. Some brood for months, years, even decades over real or imagined wrongs. Even when they no longer clearly remember exactly what their original grudge was, still they refuse to see, speak to or have anything to do with their enemy.

At a superficial glance, actions based in hatred can look similar to those motivated by evilness of wishes, a characteristic of the craving root. Damage and destruction are invariably an outcome of evilness of wishes but they're a side-effect rather than the primary intent. The craver's actions can be equally destructive and equally reprehensible but his main focus is on creation, strange though it may sound. Craving goes out and seeks contact with the environment, trying to manipulate it to produce an effect. Hatred moves away, it sets out to separate itself off from the world around.

Jack the Ripper, Cato, the monk Kappitaka, the woman with the caterpillars – their primary concern was destruction. Consider in contrast the girl who succeeded in convincing her younger siblings that they could walk on the lily-pads on the fish-pond. It wasn't that she wanted them to drown – the idea may never have crossed her mind; her interest lay rather in creating for herself an entertaining situation. Along similar lines, the Frenchwomen who sat knitting round the guillotine, the crowds who throng, ghoul-like, to the site of a road accident or plane crash – such people are attracted to disasters because they find them perversely stimulating. In their craving for sensory enjoyment, they can be quite callous about the suffering of others.

Apart from any external destruction they may cause, hate types also have a tendency to regard their own mental make-up from a negative perspective. Where cravers overrate themselves and their abilities, hate types incline towards self-deprecation. In such cases, try as you may to convince them of their sterling qualities or their first-rate skills – they'll not believe you. They know they are worthless, inadequate, even despicable.

Such an attitude – perhaps because it's confused with genuine modesty – is often felt to be OK, and this acceptance (if not approval) makes it all the more pernicious. The hate type's self-condemnation is just as reprehensible as the craver's self-praise. It's equally conceited (to consider oneself 'the worst person in the world' shows enormous self-importance) and it brings about gloom, depression, even thoughts of suicide in the individual concerned. Moreover, it can be destructive of human relationships – the self-hater just can't believe that anyone could really love him – and has a thoroughly dampening effect on the world around.

13

States of Mind: THE CONFUSED TYPE

*In one of **confused temperament** there is frequent occurrence of such states as stiffness, torpor, agitation, worry, uncertainty and clinging on tenaciously with refusal to relinquish – Visuddhi-Magga*

There was a farmer who had a herd of cows he wanted to sell. He took them to a market, clinched a satisfactory deal and walked off with a paper bag containing £14,000 in cash. Before he returned to his farm he needed to make a phone call and he absent-mindedly left his paper bag in a public phone box. As soon as he realised what he'd done he hurried back to the phone box. Someone else had got there before him and the bag was nowhere to be seen. 'It just goes to show,' the farmer was later heard to remark, 'you really can't trust people nowadays.'

Where cravers overvalue and hate types undervalue confused types simply ignore; they just don't see what's in front of them. The farmer demonstrated his confusion not only by managing to forget all about a considerable sum of money but also in the moral he drew from the incident: 'You can't trust people.' 'That was pretty stupid of me' would, you might have thought, have been a more pertinent conclusion.

Confused types view the world as if through blinkers – they ignore much of their experience, just focusing on the sometimes minimal portion in front of their eyes. Thus unaware of the larger picture, they can be quite blind as to how things hang together, how the world actually works.

You can find a similarly obtuse approach to life in the type of person who sees portents everywhere, who regards the flight of a crow through the sky as some kind of omen, who finds significance in the most trivial events and encounters. Like the farmer, such people look at the world in a peculiarly subjective way.

Confused types ignore all manner of things about themselves and the world around them. They ignore, for example, the way they look; it's not that they don't mind whether they're scruffy or not – they really don't notice. A confused type may put on someone else's clothes and wear them for some time, just not realising they're not his own. One man managed to go off to work with his wife's contact lenses in his eyes. What he knew was that he had contact lenses in – what he ignored was that they weren't as comfortable as usual nor could he see as well.

Of course cravers and hate types also ignore – they refuse to see that the courses of action they choose to follow actually bring unpleasant results. But with confused types, this not-seeing is more fundamental; ignorance, turning a blind eye, is what governs their whole approach to life.

The confused type is a drifter. He can drift from one course of action to another without even realising he's doing so. Say he's in the living room and he decides to make himself a coffee. By the time he's got to the kitchen he'll have forgotten what he's there for. He may stand there aimlessly for a few minutes, perhaps even staring at the kettle, and then go back to where he came from empty-handed.

Confused types have difficulty in keeping their minds on anything – they're as indecisive in the mental world as they are in the physical and generally are not particularly effective or productive in their work. They can spend a large proportion of their time absorbed in daydream and fantasy – because of this inability to keep their minds on what they're doing, they tend to be shoddy workers.

It often seems to be the case that confused types have no views about anything, certainly no coherent views. They simply don't know what they think about things. What's more, they're not particularly interested in knowing what they think about things. Lacking the purposefulness of cravers or hate types, they seem to lack direction; they're content to drift without ever coming to any conclusion or decision. They find it simpler to accept whatever comes their way without making any kind of assessment or enquiry. If you press them for a reason for anything, either they'll trot out the reason they heard most recently or they'll just mumble, 'I don't know.'

At a very superficial glance, you might conclude that someone who is very confused has attained that rare mental quality of equanimity – even-mindedness to whatever pain or pleasure they experience. The confused type's lack of a fixed position, his apparent willingness to go with the flow, has nothing whatsoever to do with true equanimity. One who is genuinely even-minded does not ignore – he lives in the moment, responding to each new situation with intelligent awareness.

The confused type can switch opinions in mid-sentence, blithely unaware of his inconsistency. If you show him a cup and say 'This is a red cup', he'll agree. If you then say 'Well no, it's orange really', he'll still agree. You could even tell him it was blue and he'd be likely to nod wisely, although perhaps wondering quite what you had in mind. So it's not that he won't take a position – he'll take any position at all.

If you have any dealings with a confused type, it's wise to be meticulous in making sure everything is written down, signed, sealed, notarised – whatever it takes to make sure that the details of the transaction are properly understood. There'll certainly need to be more than one copy of the document in question – if you let the confused type have the only existing copy either he'll leave it on the train or his dog will chew it up.

Most people have an element of confusion in their mental make-up – that's one of the reasons why the bureaucracy of government and the legal system has evolved as it has, with all those painfully detailed forms replete with footnotes, dependent clauses, exceptions to the rule. They aim to cut through the public's confusion by covering all possible angles and specifying every possible instance – regardless of the fact that sometimes their intricacy goes so far you'd need to be a lawyer to interpret them.

One item in the Visuddhi-Magga's list of states of mind might at first sight seem to contradict what's been said so far about the confused type's purposeless drift, and that's that rather curious phrase 'clinging on tenaciously with refusal to relinquish'. Whilst confused types might seem ultimately adaptable, able and willing to change their opinions with every wind that blows, in fact that's far from the case. Once they find an anchor, something with which they feel they can identify, they'll hang on to it like grim death.

People cling to what they're sure of, what they believe they know. They cling to things as a means of gaining some kind of personal status or identity; they cling to people, to fashions, to relationships, to philosophies, to political views, to football clubs. And in the face of all reasonable odds they keep on clinging, because they see what they cling to as themselves.

It's not uncommon, for example, to find someone voting for the party their parents supported. Never mind that the individual politicians and the policies put forward might no longer resemble in the slightest those of thirty or forty years before – they still religiously put their cross by that party. Imitation is, after all, much easier than actually thinking it all through. Not that the confused type knows he does it: he may be quite emotional about his political views, hanging on to them till the day he dies, without ever realising they were never consciously formulated as his own.

This kind of confusion can cause havoc if it spreads among a crowd. There's something about a crowd mentality that seems to bring out the confusion of the individuals. How often do people en masse imitate, sheep-like, the behaviour of their leaders, perhaps doing or saying things they would never dream of if they could think it through on their own?

An unthinking attachment to views generally lies behind any instance of mob violence. In 1582 for example, when the old Julian calendar system had got out of step with the natural seasons, developments in science and astronomy led to the decision to introduce the new and improved Gregorian calendar. To bring the vernal equinox back to March 21st, the day following October 4th was to become the 15th (rather than the 5th), thus omitting ten days from that particular year. Some people, assuming their lifespans were actually determined by the calendar, were appalled to hear some bureaucrat had deprived them of ten whole days from their lives. A public outcry arose and riots spread across Europe.

As an example of clinging at an individual level, there was a woman who became involved with a rather prestigious religious organisation. Over the years, this particular organisation went through many different phases, at one stage hitting such a low that it functioned as a home for drug-dealers and heroin addicts. While others chose to steer clear of the negative atmosphere that had developed, this woman still stayed on – she'd been there from the beginning and she didn't see why she should go. After a time the fortunes of the organisation recovered and it entered a much more positive phase. The woman was still around, now shining by the reflected glory. Up, down, positive, negative – she really didn't mind. What mattered was the sense of security her identification with the group provided.

Confused types will define themselves according to their job, their religion, their nationality, their class and they'll refuse to relinquish their hold on what they see as their identity, unable to break free of what they regard as 'themselves'.

'I'm a Pisces'/'I'm a Manchester United supporter'/'I'm a mother'/'I'm a Buddhist' – whilst such labels can of course prove convenient, each of us is in fact far more than we can possibly describe. Confused types will bind themselves to their identity and quite forget how very limited it actually is. Though circumstances change and the definition they've chosen as their identity becomes increasingly inappropriate, still will they hold on to it.

One man, for example, strongly identified with his working-class roots. When he was offered the chance to move into accommodation far more spacious than his dingy basement flat, he vehemently resisted the idea. Moreover, although he had trained as a teacher and could easily get work, he preferred to continue collecting the dole and living on the bread-line. Whilst many would have jumped at the prospect of decent accommodation and a reasonably-paid job, this man balked at what he saw as a threat to his identity, to his particular interpretation of a working-class image.

People also cling on to their habit patterns – positive or negative – and define themselves in those terms. 'I'm the sort of person who . . .' – that's a statement often heard, and it's a hallmark of the confused type. Many, for example, identify with a negative self-image. 'I'm the sort of person who always gets angry/always worries/always puts his foot in it/always gets depressed.' Clinging on to such an image, someone will cling to, say, depression, studiously ignoring any subtle change or lift in mood.

We need to bear in mind, however, that confusion – like any other mental state – is not a concrete permanent thing. Some people find they're more confused when they first get up and it takes maybe a couple of hours before the fog begins to lift. Some may be generally confused yet as sharp as a needle in specific areas – the sort of thing which gives rise to the absent-minded professor syndrome.

A group of scientists were awaiting the arrival of a man who was to give them a talk on electromagnetic radiation. When he finally appeared, he seemed very worried and upset – because somewhere in the local shopping centre, it emerged, he had managed to lose his wife (who organised his itinerary and travelled with him). Eventually the wife turned up, her husband visibly relaxed and when the meeting started he presented a very fluent and confident talk on his subject. When it came to electromagnetic radiation, he was not in the least confused; what he was confused about was life in the world outside.

Confused types often seem enveloped by an air of helplessness and general anxiety. If they should be deprived of something to cling on to, what they'll usually do is worry. Looking for a solution to their uncertainty they'll cast around – sometimes obsessively – for something solid and sure. Worry in fact solves nothing – the mind just goes round and round on the same old track, chewing away at its problems in a blinkered and unintelligent fashion. But if something comes along that offers a glimpse of light in the darkness, a hint of stability in the midst of insecurity, they seize upon it with a vice-like grip.

To try and banish all threat of the unknown from their experience, confused types will resist the fact that things change and try to turn the new into the familiar. They want a rule for every occasion, to have their life all worked out in advance. If they're invited out for dinner, they'll want to know exactly what to wear and when to arrive. If a confused type goes on some kind of course and is given a timetable which doesn't specify precisely how he should occupy himself for every minute of the day, he'll ask questions like 'But what exactly should I be doing between 10.10 and 10.15?'

Remember, though, that there are degrees of confusion – whilst those who are moderately confused may well worry a lot, someone who is extremely confused may not worry at all because he doesn't even see that there's a problem. And then there are also those who are minimally confused, who can exist in an utterly fluid situation without being thrown. For such people there can be changes happening all around but they're not bothered, they just let them happen as they will. They recognise that to cling would be the worst thing they could do, and that change is an unavoidable part of life.

14

States of Mind: THE FAITH TYPE

*In one of **faithful temperament** there is frequent occurrence of such states as free generosity, desire to see noble ones, desire to hear the good Dhamma, great gladness, ingenuousness, honesty and trust in things that inspire trust – Visuddhi-Magga*

At first glance the above list of mental attributes may not seem very relevant in modern Western society, and it can indeed be said that those qualities typically associated with faith are not particularly respected in the West today. Whilst the general bias nowadays is towards technology and materialism, the cultural milieu in which the list was formulated was strongly religious and devotional. Given that an individual is inevitably conditioned by the society in which he lives, the cultivation of those qualities derived from the faith root is less evident in the twentieth-century Westerner than it was in the Oriental of Buddhaghosa's day.

However, these qualities most certainly still exist and can be seen more readily in those societies which are based upon a

strong religious tradition. They're also prominent in the kind
of society which the West rather condescendingly terms
'primitive', where the people are more attuned to the natural
cycles of life and are still prepared to allow themselves the
luxury of such qualities as 'great gladness'.

The general consensus in the West is, unfortunately, that
qualities like ingenuousness, honesty and trust are in fact
impractical, unworldly, naïve; lovely theoretical ideas but
useless when it comes down to getting what you want out of
life. Western ideas about how to find happiness, based as they
usually are on pure materialism, are often short-sighted:
pleasure on the instant is what they aim for, regardless of any
suffering they produce in the long term. In fact, when it comes
to achieving some kind of fulfilment in life, the approach of the
positive roots – faith, intelligence and speculation – is in the
long run by far the more effective one.

Faith wants more of that which is efficient, that which leads
away from dissatisfaction and distress. It's the polar opposite
of craving – cravers also want more, but they want it for
themselves and they want it *now*. They look only to immediate
personal gain and are blind to the inefficiency of their
approach. Lacking the faith type's broader view, they don't
appreciate that the pursuit of selfish advantage can only ever
lead to unpleasant results. The craver says 'Yes please!' to
selfish pleasures; the faith type says 'Yes' to positive and
efficient qualities like compassion, generosity and honesty.

One aspect fundamental to the faith type's view of life is his
assumption that all is working entirely as it should; that
whether he understands exactly how it's working or not, it's
still the case that life's providing him with just what he needs.
He believes, in short, that the universe is benevolent. In the
words of the English mystic Julian of Norwich, 'All shall be
well and all shall be well and all manner of thing shall be well.'

That's not a particularly common attitude in the West
today. Many people have the idea that life's out to get them,

that unless they look out for themselves at every turn they're going to get hurt. They doubt that the universe has their best interests at heart – they see it as a hostile aggressive place.

A man who was a faith type was packing for a trip to India when someone asked him a question which stopped him in his tracks: 'What kind of gun are you taking?' Not 'Are you taking a gun?' – 'What kind of gun?' The man pointed out to his questioner that in his opinion, if he chose to carry weapons, that showed that he was expecting trouble and he would therefore certainly find it. He preferred not to carry a weapon, not to expect trouble and not to find it. His faith was borne out in that he travelled through some very dangerous areas but never once came to any harm.

One reason faith has something of a bad name in the West is that some people who are strong in faith are also strong in confusion. Thanks to their faith root, they desire what is efficient; but thanks to their confusion, they're not clearly aware what is actually beneficial to themselves and others, and they can thus make some disastrous mistakes. A typical example is the spiritual seeker who puts his trust in a guru who is not in fact to be trusted. Hearing tales of scandalous goings-on in ashrams and meditation centres, many a Westerner becomes sceptical about the whole idea of seeking truth, tarring every spiritual teacher with the same brush.

However, when those who have the faith and intelligence roots well developed find someone or something they really can trust, they can reap enormous rewards. Whether they're a musician, artist or spiritual seeker, if they come across a teacher whose knowledge and experience is greater than their own, they'll be prepared to put aside their own views and opinions and drink in what he or she has to tell them. The more trust they have in their teacher, the more readily they'll obey instructions and the more speedily they'll progress.

Faith is a very creative quality – faith has both vision and a belief that there is an answer to be found. This holds good whatever field we consider. There have, for example, been many scientists and doctors who held out against the scepticism of their peers and won through to great inventions and discoveries. Or consider people who work with autistic children and after months and months with seemingly no results eventually succeed in establishing a line of communication.

When it comes to questions like the purpose of life itself, someone who believes there are answers to be found will have a great respect for any religious or spiritual way which leads towards the unravelling of such mysteries, whether or not they're actively engaged in that way themselves.

A Canadian woman was living in a small village in Northern India when she heard that her Tibetan guru had died. At the time she was waiting for money to be wired through to her and didn't have enough to travel to his funeral. On the offchance, she went into the local hardware store and asked the owner whether he might consider lending her 300 rupees, which she'd calculated as being the minimum she'd need for her journey. He asked her why she wanted the money, and on hearing the magical word 'guru', he promptly presented her with twice the amount she'd asked for as an outright gift.

Generosity is another characteristic of faith types. Cravers may spend a lot of money on themselves – faith types would rather share their money, possessions or time with other people. Again, this is a quality which is particularly well developed in the Orient.

As an example, some expatriate Sri Lankans in England had offered to cook a meal for the inhabitants of a local Buddhist monastery. That week there were more visitors to the monastery than there'd ever been and the monks were rather concerned for the people who were going to do the cooking. They phoned them up and explained that there could be as many as thirty to cater for. The Sri Lankans said 'Oh good!' – they were thrilled to be able to give more than they'd expected.

Generosity is of course by no means only found in Oriental or spiritual circles. In the West, many have provided the financial support for artistic or educational ventures – founding colleges, establishing scholarships, not to speak of donations towards hospitals, hospices and other kinds of development projects.

But the common idea of giving in the West equates generosity with charity: you give to those who are poorer, more needy, in some way further down the scale than you are. Thus the kind of giving frequently found in India – epitomised in the situation where an already wealthy guru is presented with yet another Rolls-Royce – is regarded by Westerners with extreme suspicion.

The Oriental view is that through giving you form a link with the person to whom you give. An Oriental would judge it far preferable to give to one who is spiritually advanced (whether financially well-off or not). He thus aims to form positive links with the mental qualities displayed by the recipient, qualities (such as wisdom and compassion) which he seeks to develop in himself.

As faith and craving represent opposite ends of the same spectrum, you can find at the faith end extreme and relatively selfless generosity; whilst moving into the craving side you may come upon a far less pure and positive kind of giving – such as the parents who give to their children in order that they can have the best bikes on the block. Similarly, the kind of almost mandatory giving that goes on at Christmas or birthdays has little to do with the faith root – there's a family where the same ten-pound note has been passing from member to member over several years of festive occasions. Again, if you give someone a picture or piece of furniture which you never liked and which is cluttering up your house, the element of efficiency in your action is minimal.

Honesty is another quality associated with the faith root. Given their conviction that life is essentially good, faith types don't feel the need to protect themselves by lying or being economical with the truth. They haven't necessarily consciously thought it out in that way – they just naturally tend to present an open front. Whereas cravers always try to put themselves in a good light, faith types will be quite prepared to admit to failures and weaknesses in their characters.

Today those communities where doors are left unlocked are rare, and it's not uncommon for employees who don't fiddle their expenses at work to come under pressure from their colleagues to change their ways. Where getting away with what you can is all too common in modern commercial circles, faith types believe in doing a fair day's work for a fair day's pay. Generous with their time as with their money, they won't be continually trying to cut corners in their work, in contrast with their lazier craving colleagues.

One reward, as it were, of the faith type's inclination towards the efficient is that there'll be times when happiness wells up within him for no apparent reason; he feels that it's great just to be alive. Faith types generally see the positive side of situations, finding confirmation in the world around them of their view that life is good and that everything works for the best.

It's not only their own circumstances or achievements they take delight in: they also find joy in the successes of their fellows. Again, this quality – known in Buddhism as sympathetic joy – is not particularly prominent in the West. If someone wins a coveted promotion or a holiday to the Seychelles, the sort of comments his associates make are usually along the lines of 'It's all right for some!' The faith type, however, can be genuinely glad for another: he views their success as evidence of life's potential – 'If they can achieve this, I can too.'

The attitude of the faith type is well illustrated by the following story. The architect Sir Christopher Wren was touring the site where work was in progress for the construction of St Paul's Cathedral. Coming upon three men who were all engaged in the same task, he asked each of them what they were doing. The first remarked, rather brusquely: 'I'm laying bricks.' The second said: 'I'm just earning my wages.' The third man might have been living in a totally different world. He said: 'I'm helping to build a great cathedral!'

15

States of Mind: THE INTELLIGENT TYPE

*In one of **intelligent temperament** there is frequent occurrence of such states as readiness to be spoken to, possession of good friends, knowledge of the right amount in eating, mindfulness and full awareness, devotion to wakefulness, a sense of urgency about things that should inspire a sense of urgency, and wisely directed endeavour – Visuddhi-Magga*

If someone has an IQ of 160, a fistful of degrees and doctorates and membership of Mensa, do you thereby conclude that he's intelligent? In the West, most people do. The Western definition of the term tends to equate intelligence with intellectuality and the ability to acquire intellectual qualifications – which is *not* how the quality is viewed from a Buddhist standpoint.

What the Westerner assumes to be intelligence has more to do with skill at manipulating information, with a capacity to learn, recall and organise data; whether or not you comprehend the material you've amassed is another question. All you can really deduce from a high IQ is that the person has the ability to accurately complete an IQ test more speedily than most.

In the Buddhist sense, intelligence (which is the polar opposite of hatred) is seen rather as a measure of a person's ability to make right links and connections; to assess a situation from an objective perspective and take appropriate action. The mark of the intelligent type is that he has the capacity to judge which actions will prove to be ultimately beneficial and to discard those which will not, those which will lead to his own or others' distress. The hate type, operating from an essentially self-centred viewpoint, lacks this kind of detachment and discrimination and aims to discard just about anything.

Unblinkered by the kind of passions that urge cravers and hate types to try and turn the world to their own immediate advantage, the outlook intelligent types adopt is cooler, less egocentric. They're clearly aware that the world is a very dynamic place, a place of flux and change. Because they know that new things are forever coming into being, that whatever worldly knowledge and skills they acquire will sooner or later become outmoded, they know they have no choice but to be adaptable. Where the negative roots can often be dogmatic in their approach, fixed in their outlook, intelligent types are always ready to re-assess in the light of new information.

Aware of the infinite extent of knowledge to be had, an intelligent type would never claim a monopoly, whatever his field of study. What he wants is to understand, and he's quite prepared to accept that there are others who know more than he does himself – which means that he doesn't resist correction. He has no problems in admitting that someone else's skill is greater than his own; that it's worth listening to another individual and learning from his experience.

Think of any evening class you've attended: whatever the subject of study – Italian, upholstery, public-speaking,

Buddhist meditation – there'll always be some people in the class who obviously hate to be wrong. They become very defensive if their errors are pointed out, quite forgetting that they only enrolled in the first place because they wanted to understand. Intelligent types are not like that. Omniscience plays no part in their self-image – they're quite happy to admit their own lack of knowledge and that way they learn far more readily.

Their ability to discriminate means that they can be selective about their friends. They recognise that to associate with people whose views are diametrically opposed to their own will bring them no profit. The reformed gambler or drug addict, for example, will if he has any intelligence avoid his former companions. And where cravers like to mix with the rich and the famous for the kudos they think they derive from such company, intelligent types are able to see through the lure of reflected glory. They don't, like hate types, discard people altogether – they're just careful to avoid those who'll interfere with their drive towards minimising distress.

'Knowledge of the right amount in eating' may at first sight seem a rather peculiar characteristic to isolate. However, food occupies a central position in any human life – after all, there can't be life without it – and the way an individual responds to food serves as an accurate indicator of their response to sensuality in general.

Many people are unskilful in their attitude to food, particularly in the West. Increased affluence means that eating is not just a matter of survival – it can become a psychological obsession, as in conditions like anorexia and bulimia. Many are caught on the pendulum that swings between greed and self-chosen deprivation, and between them the food industry and the slimming industry – with its special diets, special drinks and food products, special exercise techniques – have a vested interest in keeping that pendulum swinging.

Intelligent types take a sensible approach to food; they avoid obsession by finding a middle path between the extremes of gluttony and starvation. They discard both overeating and undereating, recognising that either will impair their effectiveness in functioning in the world. They see nothing wrong with enjoying the food they do eat, but they know when they've had enough.

In other areas of sensuality the intelligent type's approach will be similarly balanced. Some people (invariably cravers) become obsessed by music: they will put on the same record again and again and again, hoping to perpetuate the enjoyment they derive from it. As well as infuriating all those within earshot, they invariably find that the power of the music to provide them with pleasure diminishes rapidly, leaving them feeling jaded and dissatisfied. Whether it's food, music, art, television or sex, intelligent types recognise the value of moderation, of controlling their sensual appetites rather than being controlled by them.

They also practise moderation in the matter of sleep. They realise that sleeping the day away is a waste of time and usually leads to dullness and lethargy; and that habitually making do on three or four hours' a night will equally impair their functioning.

They're always keen to learn and they know that the best way to learn is through observation of experience. As they want to develop wisdom, they know they're going to considerably reduce their chances if they spend a lot of time escaping into unconsciousness or daydream. For best results, they need to be fully awake and also fully attentive.

If they want to learn about people, for example, they'll pay close attention to the ways people behave. They'll also recognise that gathering intellectual information by reading books or asking questions of those who know more than they do themselves is a sensible way to speed up the process. They know that if they read a book about, say, body language, and then observe what they see around them, the combination of study and experience invariably proves the most effective route to understanding.

When it comes to dealing with people, intelligent types make fine negotiators and resolvers of conflicts, able as they are to detach themselves from any passionate involvement and view the disagreements that bedevil many human relationships from an unbiased perspective. And they take their responsibilities seriously: they understand that responsibility of some kind is part and parcel of the human condition and without it one can't attain one's full potential.

Bear in mind that this system of character analysis is a very dynamic one. The Western approach to intelligence as measured by the IQ suggests that it is a given quality, one which cannot be radically adjusted, adapted or changed throughout a lifetime. It assumes that you're born with a certain level of intelligence and you also die with it, except insofar as it's eroded in the process of ageing.

Buddhism understands that everything is in a state of constant change. Mental qualities, whether positive or negative, never stand still; you can train yourself to be inefficient, you can train yourself to be efficient. Intelligence is increased when we start to observe suffering rather than trying always to evade it.

The life of Richard Randall, one of the pioneers of Buddhism in Britain, graphically demonstrates this principle. Up until his mid-forties, Richard Randall had immersed himself in an academic study of the Buddhist teaching, regularly and enthusiastically lecturing on the subject. One night, during a lecture in Oxford, he was describing to his audience how vital it was to test out the Buddha's philosophy by putting the theories into practice. Suddenly it struck him that this was something that he'd never done himself, that for all his erudition and enthusiasm his knowledge of Buddhism remained purely intellectual.

'Gentlemen,' he informed his audience, 'I am a fraud.' The next day he embarked whole-heartedly upon the course he had long advocated to others but never followed himself. He left behind his home, his family, and his business and made arrangements to travel immediately to a Buddhist country where he might find instruction on how to put the teaching into practice. In a temple near Bangkok, he took at the age of forty-seven the radical step of ordaining as a monk and devoted himself to the practice of meditation.

In keeping with their awareness of the flux and flow of life, intelligent types know that no one can tell what the future holds. Accordingly, they feel it's important to really commit themselves to whatever activity they're engaged in if they're going to get the most out of it. Where cravers tend to put things off, under the assumption that they have all the time in the world, intelligent types recognise that time is short and they thus develop a real sense of urgency, of dedication to the task in hand.

This quality is particularly critical in the search for spiritual understanding. A person whose intelligence root is weak may get caught up in mundane concerns, reasoning that when he gets a less stressful job or his divorce comes through or his health improves – that's when he'll *really* get down to meditation and study. But one whose intelligence is strong wouldn't dream of waiting for more favourable conditions: he's acutely aware that he might die or his teacher might die and that it only makes sense to work hard while he can.

There are many examples of spiritual seekers who have taken this approach. There's a story in the Pali Canon about a man called Bahiya who came to hear that a Buddha, an enlightened being, had arisen in the world. The very day he heard the news he set off on a journey over hundreds of miles to the place where the Buddha was staying. When he arrived at the monastery, he was told that the Buddha was somewhere in town, walking on his almsround. Bahiya immediately began searching the streets and eventually came upon him.

The Buddha initially refused Bahiya's request for instruction, the almsround not being the most conducive of teaching situations. Bahiya's sense of urgency drove him to persist and at his third request the Buddha recognised his dedication by speaking a few brief words. Such was Bahiya's spiritual maturity that those words were enough to lead him to enlightenment.

The approach of the intelligent type is perhaps summed up in the quality of 'wisely directed endeavour'. However committed someone may be to a task, if he's not able to direct his efforts in a sensible way they'll inevitably misfire. Intelligent types make good use of the resources they have available to them. Their sense of urgency enables them to establish their priorities in life and within that context, they're able to apply the energy they have in a consistent and balanced way.

It may mean that at times they'll decide to head straight for their goal (Bahiya, incidentally, was gored to death by a cow within hours of attaining enlightenment). There may equally be occasions when they'll bide their time, aware that wait-and-see may be a more appropriate strategy than diving headlong in. If, for example, they need to reprimand someone or break some bad news, neither will they act at the first opportunity nor will they bury their heads in the sand by continually putting it off. They'll know when the time is right and they'll have the patience to wait until it is.

The aim of the intelligent type is always towards the positive. He invariably tries to act in such a way as to minimise suffering – not just the suffering in his own life but also that of his fellows. Recognising the interdependence of all beings, he is aware that to aspire exclusively towards his own happiness just doesn't work. And when the efficiency of intelligence combines with the warmth of faith, there results an individual who is strong in compassion and potentially a great force for good in the world.

16

States of Mind: THE SPECULATIVE TYPE

*In one of **speculative temperament** there is frequent occurrence of such states as talkativeness, sociability, boredom with devotion to the profitable, failure to finish undertakings, smoking by night and flaming by day, and mental running hither and thither –*
Visuddhi-Magga

Speculation is a very expansive quality – in essence it's the wish to find answers, to formulate theories, to plan, experiment, design, create. Confusion, the polar opposite of speculation, has no interest in questioning and investigating. Confused types stay firmly glued to what they know, whilst speculators move outward in search of the new. Where confused types plump for familiar routine, speculators are always prepared to entertain new possibilities. They take a look at what's currently on offer and ask 'How would it be if we tried it *this* way?'

What both types have in common is a tendency to be indecisive – the confused type may not even recognise there's a decision to be made; the speculator's discursiveness sees so many possible solutions that he finds it difficult to narrow the options down.

Speculators want answers to the questions they pose; they want to know the hows, the whys, the wherefores. 'How do migrating birds navigate?' 'Why do Swiss Cheese plants have holes in their leaves?' 'How does fluoride help prevent tooth decay?' 'Why is there a correlation between sunspot activity and the state of the stock market?' These are all typical speculative questions – speculators have a natural curiosity about the world and questions will occur to them which many would just never have thought of asking.

This love of enquiry for enquiry's sake has been the driving force behind so much of human achievement. Without it, society simply stagnates. The desire to move into new territory, to seek out new ways of doing things, to investigate both the internal and external environment, has led to all kinds of discoveries. Exploration of unknown lands, space travel, developments in technology, medicine, education and the arts – new ventures in whatever field require people of vision, those with the ability to dream up the ideas which one day can be transformed into physical realities.

Speculation is a quality that is essential for the expansion of knowledge and the development of wisdom (whether in the worldly or the spiritual sense) and thus is most certainly a positive root. However, if speculation goes unchecked, it can proliferate endlessly; the questions multiply and the thinking circles round and round with never a solid conclusion in sight.

For speculative types, there is always an infinite supply of questions to ask and an infinite variety of theories to postulate. It is, after all, in the nature of speculation: the more you think about something, the more possibilities do you become aware of. Because it has this tendency to get out of hand, speculation unchecked may veer off in a less than positive direction – as some of the qualities listed above suggest.

Speculators thrive on mental stimulation. They're never happier than when they're receiving new input and accordingly they're usually rather social animals. Conversation provides a natural outlet for the expression of their thoughts. Mixing with others gives them the opportunity to hear new ideas, to share their own theories and develop them further dependent on the feedback they receive. Where confused types shrink from moves towards innovation, regarding the new as a potential threat to their present security, speculators are generally very open to new ideas, new schemes and suggestions.

Because they can get so caught up in thinking, spending much of their time in the heady world of hypothesis and the imagination, speculators do have trouble coming down to earth and applying themselves to mundane repetitive tasks. Where there's no room for theorising, for expansion, for building castles in the air, speculators soon become bored.

'Boredom with devotion to the profitable' refers specifically to the attempt to practise mindfulness and meditation. Meditation is essentially an exercise in moment-by-moment observation of experience, gathering facts about how things operate; it is *not* thinking about the facts you've gathered, how things might operate if given a free rein. Meditation is concerned with the restraint of planning and thinking rather than their proliferation. As such, it's the antithesis of speculation.

Because they're easily bored, speculators may be quick to turn their sights to another direction before they've finished the job in hand. Whether we're talking about mental work like meditation or tasks of a more physical nature, speculators may apply their energies inconsistently and unsteadily, lacking the perseverance to make it through to the end.

One meditative trainee with a speculative bent was instructed to go out and dig the garden – to him a mundane repetitive task if ever there was one. Before he'd even put hand to spade his mind was skating off in search of stimulation. 'There's a parallel here,' he thought to himself, 'between what Bennett was told to do by Gurdjieff; he got some pretty interesting experiences out of it. So if I just shovel earth around for a moment or two I expect I'll come up with something similar.' In fact what he got was boredom rather than interest, and not much movement of earth.

The creativity involved in planning or design is especially appealing to speculators. When faced with a logistical problem, they'll think things through and come up with viable and imaginative solutions. The organisation of something like the Olympic Games, for example, requires speculative planning of the most skilful and intricate kind: organising people, locations, schedules; juggling possibilities and probabilities; detecting and coming up with solutions to all kinds of potential problems.

Of course, a speculator could equally set his planning tendencies to work upon a totally hypothetical situation, wherein they could work on endlessly and to little point. There are countless bar-room politicians who've decided exactly how they would handle the latest economic crisis; and quite a few writers of novels that will never be published who have worked out how much they'll ask for the film rights and which stars they'd like to cast in the leading roles.

Speculators will, as the Visuddhi-Magga says, 'smoke by night and flame by day'. In other words at night-time, when they're unable to act, they'll plot and scheme, build plan upon plan; then when daylight comes it's 'Right – let's get to it!' And they rush round in a whirlwind of activity trying to implement all of the ingenious ideas they came up with the night before.

It's important to remember that you will never come across anyone who is motivated solely by speculation – there's always going to be a mixture of the roots, with one or maybe two predominant. However, in order to try and get at the pure expression, the essence of the root in question, it's necessary to present something of a caricature.

To be effective and truly efficient, speculation really needs to be aligned with intelligence. Intelligence brings speculation down to earth. Where speculation comes up with a mass of possible conclusions, intelligence will cut through to the meat of the matter and throw out those which are inefficient, unworkable or inappropriate. Speculation alone doesn't have the necessary discrimination. It may lead, for example, to the mad inventor syndrome, where people come up with the most ridiculous contraptions that no one would ever conceive of putting to practical use. The ideas may be sound enough – they're just lacking in common-sense.

When it comes to the spiritual search, speculation and intelligence form an extremely powerful combination. The exploration of the nature of reality holds a keen fascination for the speculator; intelligence keeps him on track, cutting through his tendency to indulge in purely intellectual theorising. Questions like 'How many angels can stand on the point of a needle?' will not grab such an individual's interest. His questioning will not spin off into thin air but will ground itself on the actual facts of his mental and physical experience.

The root of speculation has been strong in many of history's greatest minds. The capacity for creativity, visualisation and experiment, for example, is particularly fundamental to the world of science. Leonardo da Vinci conceived of and designed helicopters and submarines centuries before they were to become a physical reality. Earlier still, Roger Bacon, an English philosopher of the thirteenth century, had suggested that one day there would be flying-machines and motorised ships and carriages.

In the sixteenth century, his namesake, Francis Bacon, played a key role in the introduction of a systematic and objective approach to scientific method, employing the intelligence-speculation combination of roots to great effect. One of his proposals was the establishment of a vast complex – including a library of all books in all known languages, a botanical gardens, a comprehensive zoo, a museum and a laboratory for experimental research – so that the heavens and earth could be studied, observed and classified in a scientific way. Science, he claimed, should be known by its fruits – not by endless theorising. He later suggested the foundation of a college of inventors, complete with pensions for research workers, allowances for travel and experiments, libraries, laboratories and scientific prizes.

He also made proposals in the political arena, producing reams of draft documents and recommendations for improving King James's revenue, as well as suggesting government reforms to encourage the introduction and development of manufacturing industries.

But his primary interest was science. In March 1626, as his carriage drove through the snow of Highgate village, he was pondering about the properties of heat when he was suddenly struck with an idea about the possibilities of using snow as a preservative. He leapt from his carriage, bought a chicken from a farmer's wife and stuffed it with snow to test out his theory. There's no record of the fate of the chicken – Bacon himself caught a chill from which he never recovered.

17

BUDDHIST CHARACTER ANALYSIS
& THE SPIRITUAL PATH

In order to set this form of character analysis in the context of the spiritual path, it's necessary first to give an outline of the Buddhist teaching. In fact the Buddha himself provided a beautifully concise summary in four statements known as the four noble truths.

The first truth states that there is suffering or distress – that life in the relative world is fundamentally unsatisfactory. Hearing this, and taking no account of the other three truths, some have jumped to the conclusion that the Buddhist outlook is essentially a pessimistic one. The Buddha, however, never denied that happiness could be found in the world – he just pointed out that if we expect that happiness to last, to provide permanent satisfaction, we're going to be sadly disappointed. No matter on what grounds happiness arises – possessions, people, wealth, desirable mental states – inevitably they will age, decay and die, as will the happiness that arose dependent upon them.

The second truth states that suffering has a cause, an origin. It's not something that falls upon us out of the blue – we become dissatisfied whenever we desire things to be different from the way they are right now. Whether we're wishing we had another partner or another job, or whether we're wishing there was calmness in the mind rather than agitation, we're craving to experience something other than what is actually present here and now, and it's our action of craving that brings about our mental distress.

The third truth neatly counteracts any accusations of pessimism by revealing that we don't have to keep on suffering. There is a solution to the problem – there is Nibbana, the cessation of all distress. It is also described as the destruction of craving, hatred and ignorance; the termination of the round of rebirth; enlightenment; the final refuge.

And, with the logic and precision that are typical of the Buddhist teaching, the fourth truth lays down the means by which this ultimate goal can be attained – the Buddha called it the noble eightfold path, a middle way between the extremes of indulgence and self-mortification.

This path falls into three divisions – ethical conduct, mental development and understanding or wisdom. If we avoid inefficient physical and verbal actions – actions, that is, which are motivated by the roots of craving, hatred and confusion and which inevitably result in suffering – our minds become calmer. With calmer minds, we become increasingly aware of the mental actions we perform and can thus choose to restrain craving, hatred and confusion as they arise in the mind. And once the mind is thus balanced and relatively free of negativity, unbiased observation becomes possible, allowing us clearly to see the true nature of experience.

It then becomes possible to observe the three marks or characteristics by which all mental and physical phenomena can be identified: they are all transient, unsatisfactory and devoid of any discrete controlling entity or self. When the mind has truly seen these three marks at the most profound experiential level, it gives up its search for happiness in the relative world and seeks enlightenment, the beyond.

* * *

Buddhism distinguishes two levels of truth – the mundane and the supramundane – and those who pursue the Buddhist path must work on both levels if the goal of enlightenment is to be attained.

The mundane world is the world of beings, the world of time and space, the world where people are born, grow old and die. Mundane wisdom is concerned with how to get the best out of life on that level – it's understanding about people and how they interact, how to live in harmony with others. Such understanding is necessary in some degree if our minds are to become sufficiently balanced to penetrate through to the supramundane.

Beneath the superficial reality of the relative mundane world lies the supramundane. Here there are no beings, no time, no space, but simply the arising and passing away of discrete objects, physical and mental. These are what Buddhism terms the ultimates of experience – raw data stripped of all concepts and interpretations: sounds, sights, physical sensations, thoughts, feelings. It's only at this ultimate level that the three marks can be seen with the necessary penetration – supramundane wisdom is the understanding of the transient, unsatisfactory and non-self nature of even these ultimates of experience.

Buddhist character analysis falls under the domain of the mundane level of truth: it provides a description of human beings – how they behave and what motivates their behaviour. Learning about the system and putting it into practice is a sure route to increased wisdom about the ways of the mundane world.

One aspect of the Buddhist teaching which is fundamental to understanding the operation of the mundane world is the law of *kamma*, which states that any action performed with a sense of self will have a result. Inefficient actions, where self-concern is uppermost, yield unpleasant results; efficient actions yield pleasant results. If an individual constantly indulges in sarcasm, for example, he'll find that people will tread warily round him or avoid him altogether. If he learns to restrain his penchant for cutting remarks, his associates will begin to relax in his company and feel warmer towards him. All actions, efficient or inefficient, have results.

Inseparably connected with the law of *kamma* is the principle of rebirth, the doctrine of many lifetimes, with death in one life preceding birth in the next. Kammic actions do not always yield their fruit immediately but must wait until appropriate conditions are present. Given the countless efficient and inefficient actions we have performed, the circumstances of any one lifetime can never provide the necessary support for all potential fruits to arise. It's the force of our kammic actions which keeps the wheel of rebirth turning, carrying us on to future lives.

Buddhism distinguishes thirty-one planes of existence, on any of which a being may take rebirth. They range from the hell realms, the realms of ghosts and of animals, to the highest and most refined heavens. Pain is the predominant experience in the lower realms, pleasure in the higher. In the human realm, which lies roughly in the middle, we experience a mixture of the two.

What determines the plane on which a being is reborn is quite simply the nature of his past actions. If he's performed predominantly selfish inefficient actions, he may well find himself in a painful state, perhaps in an actual hell; if he's always tried his best to act in the interests of others, he may find himself in heaven. But whether we're talking about hells, heavens or the human realm, he'll find his citizenship is only a temporary one. When the particular kammic forces that propelled him there are exhausted, the wheel of rebirth turns once more and moves him on.

In this context, the Visuddhi-Magga presents a theory originally proposed in another commentarial work, the Vimutti-Magga, about what makes an individual a particular character type:

*One of **craving temperament** has formerly had plenty of desirable tasks and gratifying work to do, or has reappeared here after dying in a heaven.*
*And one of **hating temperament** has formerly had plenty of stabbing and torturing and brutal work to do, or has reappeared here after dying in one of the hells or the Naga (serpent) existences.*
*And one of **confused temperament** has formerly drunk a lot of intoxicants and neglected learning and questioning, or has reappeared here after dying in the animal existence.*

It certainly makes sense: the craver, descending from a realm where pleasure predominates, inclines towards the good things in life; the hate type, moving upwards from a painful realm, is accustomed to focus principally on the unpleasant; and in the case of the confused type, the thoughtful approach – which could be regarded as the hallmark of the human – is one that does not come easily.

Basically, what makes anyone a particular character type is past action (and the past can be a previous lifetime, or the past of this present life). If in the past you've put a lot of energy into criticism of others, for example, then you will find that you've built up a strong tendency to practise criticism. It's become a real skill for you, something you could do in your sleep – you can see the faults in everything around you without even trying. Or so it may seem: closer examination will reveal that this fault-finding doesn't in fact happen spontaneously – it's *always* volitional. Criticism being a form of hatred, you've made yourself a hate type simply by practising hatred.

An understanding of the principle of *kamma* and result shows us how dynamic our situation actually is. It shows us also how we can within a particular lifetime change around the balance of our character roots. We can, if we so choose, train in positive traits and train out negative ones.

In addition to the insights we gain into our own mental make-up, character analysis also increases our understanding of other people. In human relationships, distress so often arises when people behave unpredictably or in ways we think they shouldn't. We're surprised and upset because we just didn't realise that they had the potential for actions of that kind. Through learning about character analysis, about the different roots and the various kinds of behaviour that derive from them, we come to understand people better; and the better we understand them, the less likely we are to be shocked or distressed by the things they say or do.

For example: cravers are not punctual. Invite a couple of cravers round for a meal and they may well be up to an hour or two late. If you're unaware of this particular trait, you can get very upset waiting for them to arrive, with time ticking by and the food drying up in the oven. When the doorbell finally rings your mood is not the most appropriate for an enjoyable evening and you'll inwardly seethe at their flow of plausible excuses – work finished late, the car wouldn't start, they lost their way . . .

Whereas once you get to know about character types, you'll make allowances, you'll anticipate the delay. If you've invited them for eight, you'll plan for the meal to be ready a good hour or so later. And when they do turn up, you'll be amused rather than annoyed by the predictability of their excuses, and the evening won't be spoiled by unnecessary friction.

*   *   *

When it comes to analysing others (and indeed ourselves), it's important to realise that there's a distinction to be made between an objective assessment and a value judgement. If we see someone frowning and glaring and crashing things around, we can be fairly safe in concluding that their current mental state is one of hatred. Such a conclusion is a perfectly accurate and objective assessment based on the facts that we've observed. But should we then proceed to start chuntering on about what a terrible person they are, always irritable and moody, how much it gets on our nerves, we've fallen headlong into value judgement.

Value judgement, unlike assessment, has nothing to do with unbiased observation – it's all very subjective, bound up with our opinions about what qualities should or should not be present in an individual. Assessment says 'Hatred is present'; value judgement says 'That person's full of hatred and it really annoys me. They should do something about it!'

It's important to make a distinction between the facts we observe about people and the opinions we hold about those facts. The more accurately and objectively we learn to assess, the less will we be distressed by others' behaviour and the smoother will our relationships become. Being more realistic about people, we no longer expect the impossible from them nor do we condemn them for the things they do. Having seen the various roots operating within our own mental make-up, we begin to realise that the forces at work within other people are the same as the forces that motivate our own behaviour – it's just a question of degree – and thus we inevitably become more tolerant, more compassionate and life takes on a greater sense of ease and harmony.

But however much we adjust and improve our relationships, however closely we guard our own behaviour, we'll find that there's always more that could be done. The process of refinement is potentially never-ending and suffering will corrupt even the most enjoyable and harmonious life we can create. Apart from anything else, we can always be certain that death will come to interrupt whatever peace and stability we've gained.

18

BUDDHIST CHARACTER ANALYSIS
& MEDITATION

The complete ending of suffering is not to be found in any adjustments we might make to the mundane world, the world of beings and their interaction. Whilst increased skill in living will lead to a more settled and happier mind, if what we seek is enlightenment then sooner or later we're going to have to shift our focus to the supramundane, the level of moment-by-moment experience. Paying attention at this level makes it possible to observe those three characteristics that are true of all phenomena: impermanence, unsatisfactoriness and non-self. Deep insight into one of these marks forms the gateway to the beyond.

Paying attention to the way things are may sound simple enough in theory; in practice it's not so easy. Our minds lack the necessary subtlety to tackle the task in the correct way, and the purpose of meditation is to gain that subtlety by observing what we do and learning how it affects us.

When it comes to the spiritual path and meditation each character type has a quite distinct approach. A good meditation teacher will have an accurate idea of the kind of problems meditators of each of the types will face, the kind of mistakes they will habitually make in their practice, and thus he will be able to provide guidance and advice specifically tailored to individual students. Given the difficulties in analysing one's own character, the student if left to his own devices may well misassess himself and accordingly misdirect his meditation.

How do **cravers** approach meditation? As always, they go for pleasure and generally tend to steer their practice towards that end – towards calm concentrated states. Physically they're usually quite relaxed, and their attachment to the pleasantly liquid feel of a body at ease – especially when coupled with their tendency to avoid anything resembling hard work – can mean that for some at least of their practice period they're gently nodding off towards sleep. Their laziness will also mean that they often find it too much trouble to remain sufficiently attentive and their meditation may become somewhat amorphous, albeit pleasurable.

When they get the balance of energy right, however, they can withdraw from the five physical senses with relative ease. Some may be sufficiently skilled in concentration to enter the *jhana*, those states where the mind is fixed upon a single object; most, however, will tend to concentrate in a less disciplined way and will experience the vivid mental pictures and fantastic imagery that can arise when the level of alertness is not sufficient for the level of concentration. In either case, cravers are liable to become attached to concentrated states of mind, and their capacity for concentration can lead to great problems with conceit.

A craver wants stimulating experiences – he's not particularly keen on study (again, it's too much like hard work). He is attracted to the colourful exotica often associated with meditation: candles, incense, gongs, ceremonies, silk robes embroidered with mystic symbols. His acquisitiveness will induce him to collect spiritual badges of one sort or another – maybe meditation courses with prestigious teachers, maybe an endless succession of initiations or empowerments. A craver can also be something of an evangelist and, ever confident in his own abilities, may go so far as to set up his own centre or group. In the right circles, he's certainly not above using the fact that he meditates as some kind of credential.

His high opinion of his own attainments means that he tends to overvalue his experiences and overestimate his own progress. When discussing his meditation with his teacher, he will try to project a very good image of himself; the picture he presents may well be rather rosier than the truth warrants. He's not necessarily being deliberately deceitful – he may be quite unaware of the way he's adjusting the facts.

Quickly glossing over or omitting altogether anything he regards as less than successful, he reports either what he thinks the teacher wants to hear, or what he thinks the teacher should hear. A skilful teacher, however, knows how to read between the lines. The instructions offered will be aimed at the heart of the problem: the root of craving.

Meditation is not separate from life – the mind with which we meditate is not different from the mind with which we approach any other activity – and accordingly the scope of a spiritual teacher's instructions will often range beyond the limits of the seated practice as such.

In the days of the Visuddhi-Magga, if a monk sought his teacher's guidance on curbing craving, he might be advised to wear old coarse robes or to choose as his dwelling place a dilapidated hut in bleak surroundings, in order to loosen his attachment to sensual pleasures. Circumstances are rather different for a twentieth-century lay-person but the principle remains the same. Cravers today may be advised to spend less on clothes, not to eat so much, to keep their eyes restrained when they're walking down the street.

A teacher will also suggest that a craver combats his habitual laziness by learning to apply more effort to his practice. He needs to become systematic and self-disciplined, meditating on a regular daily basis rather than just when he's in the mood.

To come to understanding, cravers have to learn to see the disadvantages of the objects they crave for. If a meditator speaks in glowing terms of the wonderful visions he experiences in his practice – strange faces perhaps, or mandalas or Buddha figures – his teacher (being well aware that in 99% of cases such 'visions' are sheer fantasy) will try to counteract his attachment by pointing out how transient they are. He will stress that the fact of their impermanence is their only relevance to the meditator.

Monks in the Buddha's day who had problems with lust were directed towards the local charnel ground where meditation based on the sight of a bloated or rotting corpse would help instill a more accurate picture of the true nature of the body. Contemplating the inevitability of death is a specific practice that a teacher will often recommend to a craving student. To recollect how death comes to all is an excellent way of counteracting the craver's feeling that he has all the time in the world. He reminds himself that it's impossible to tell how, when and where death will strike, and thus arouses within himself a sense of urgency, a desire to get on with the meditation while he has the opportunity.

Where for cravers the primary goal is pleasure – which some will seek through concentration, others perhaps through taking it easy or being seen as 'good meditators' – what **hate types** want out of the meditation is peace and quiet. They believe that by getting rid of things they can achieve an untroubled state free of all pressures. This idea is a powerful myth in the psyche of the hate type – they want nothing more than to be left alone in peace. Quietude, however, can never be achieved through the exercise of hatred. In practice, hate types employ far too much force to achieve their end and only succeed in generating even more tension. As a result, in meditation their bodies are generally painful, particularly around the neck, back and shoulders, and as they try ever harder, the pains can reach an excruciating pitch.

Meditators are instructed not to move during their hour of practice, as to still the body helps to still the mind. Whilst cravers may tell themselves it's only sensible to shift around just a little, perhaps to ease a crick in the neck, hate types will take the instruction absolutely literally. Ever stoical in their approach, they won't move a muscle throughout the whole period and their bodies can sometimes seem to quiver with the tension of it all.

Time moves slowly for hate types. Impatience is a common form of hatred and when impatience is present, the mind is continually jumping forward to the end of the session and an hour can seem a very long time indeed.

Hate types are usually alert – perhaps too alert. Unlike cravers, they don't have much trouble being mindful and attentive – their difficulty lies in settling the mind sufficiently to develop calm and concentration. Whilst their bodies may not move, their minds can be hives of activity. They're continually analysing, trying to find out exactly what's going on so that they can knock it all into what they consider to be the required shape.

In their attempt to gain concentration, they'll want to force out anything they regard as an obstacle. They may consider the gurgling of a radiator or the rhythmical snoring of the meditator in the next seat a real intrusion into their practice and attempt to drive all sounds out of their minds. True concentration is never won by force. The mind becomes concentrated when it learns to repeatedly, patiently and gently withdraw from the world around. All the hate type's tactics can ever yield is agitation, mental and physical rigidity – and a yet stronger tendency towards hatred.

Self-discipline isn't usually a problem for hate types. Given their tunnel-visioned approach, they tend to regard the seated practice as the sole means to attain the goal of enlightenment; they'll be inclined to meditate all the hours available and more besides. They usually steer clear of groups, preferring to practise on their own, and can see no point in the paraphernalia of incense and gongs that so appeal to cravers. They have a predilection for asceticism and delight at the prospect of giving things up, whether it's food, sleep or sex.

They're usually not averse to study and if they apply to their own practice some of the instructions they come across without seeking guidance from a teacher, they may find themselves in deep waters. For whilst the Buddha's teaching is universally applicable, it contains many specific instructions which are directed primarily towards cravers.

As a huge generalisation, craving is the predominant root among natives of hot climates, whilst in colder climates the natives are more likely to gravitate towards hatred. People from hot countries tend on the whole to be more volatile, emotional, sociable, lazy and fond of all the good things in life. Those from colder climates tend to be more ruthless and aggressive; they can be very disciplined and hard-working and emotionally controlled.

Northern India where the Buddha lived and taught is certainly one of the hotter areas of the world and very broadly speaking, the majority of his students would have been cravers. Many of the instructions he gave were designed to curb the craver's habitual laziness by encouraging him to apply more energy and increase his determination and self-discipline.

Try shipping the Buddha's teaching wholesale to the West, to the colder regions where the hate root is more prominent, and you can run into problems. More effort, more discipline, stricter rule-keeping, ascetic practices: the hate type will find such instructions very appealing – they're just the sort of things he likes to do already. Of course, the harder he strives, the more excessive does his habit of over-effort become and the more painful and unrewarding the whole procedure.

The Buddha taught a middle way. He taught that it is both possible and indeed necessary to tread a path between the extremes of indulgence in pleasure and a ruthless subjugation of the sensual appetites. To arrive at that middle way, different character types need to approach it from different directions, and the clear vision of a skilful teacher is invaluable in indicating the correct line of approach.

When the hate type meets with his teacher, the picture he presents of his meditation can be just as distorted as the craver's, but where the craver will seize upon and magnify the least spark of apparent success, the hate type will be quite dismissive of the positive aspects of his practice. Even if for fifty minutes of an hour's session his mind was relatively calm, his report will focus on those few rather tricky moments where tension, restlessness and impatience were uppermost. In keeping with his strong perfectionist streak, he may lament on how far short his meditation falls from the ideal to which he aspires.

A competent teacher will do his best to counteract the hate type's habitual tendency to view the world in a negative light, to regard the path of meditation as a grim uphill slog. He'll suggest that his student learn to be gentler in his approach. He'll advise him to take time out to relax the body, for example, before turning the mind towards the meditation object, rather than instantly forcing the mind on to it. He may encourage him to get more in touch with his senses and point out that there's nothing wrong in enjoying sensory experience – it's only a problem if he becomes attached to it. He'll remind his student that meditation is all about accepting what is present – whether it be physical or mental pain, sleepiness or anxiety – and that the hate type's attempt to destroy present experience can only aggravate the situation.

Or tackling the problem from the outside in, the teacher may, for example, instruct his student to stop walking so heavily and banging doors, to increase the size of his hand-writing or to wear more colourful clothes. He will stress that there's more to the spiritual path than the seated practice alone, and suggest that he'd be wise to spend some time with his family rather than forever trying to shut himself away in meditation. Such self-centred ambition will only increase his sense of isolation.

One specific antidote for hatred is *metta* or loving-kindness meditation, which aims to cultivate a feeling of friendliness for all beings and as such can prove an invaluable aid to an individual determined to curb the hatred within his character. *Metta* also develops the quality of patience and can make great inroads into the hate type's joyless and teeth-gritted approach.

Meditation is something with which a predominantly **confused type** of character will find great difficulty. What the confused type wants to do is to ignore, to avoid seeing what's actually going on. He refuses to consider problems, often even failing to recognise that a problem exists. Meditation aims in the opposite direction: its purpose is to increase rather than dull our awareness of the present moment.

The confused type may drift through his hour's practice in something of a haze – exactly as he drifts through life. Where the craver is just too lazy to pay attention, the confused type is virtually unable to. Rare will be the occasions when his mind will settle on the meditation object – its habitual tendency is to scatter and meander all over the place, and its general tone is dull and muddled.

Sleepiness is common among confused types. In accord-ance with their desire to ignore, they try to plunge into the abyss of unconsciousness. Not that such a course of action is consciously chosen: confused types are rarely sufficiently aware of their own motivations to act in a deliberate or purposeful way. Of course, it's not only confused types who experience sleep in meditation – cravers may be too lazy to stay alert and awake; hate types can drive themselves unconscious by their over-forceful attempts at concentration.

When the confused type comes to give a meditation report, his teacher needs patience – lots of it. Seeing the student doesn't really know what's been going on in his mind, to put his experience into words is not easy. Each sentence will seem to take nearly a minute to emerge and when it does it's full of ums and ers and disclaimers and provisos.

If someone has a lot of confusion in their character, it's suggested in the Visuddhi-Magga that there's no point in teaching them meditation to any degree, simply because they really won't be able to understand or follow the instructions. If they should learn meditation, rather than the seated practice they'd be better off devoting their time to walking meditation, to observing the feelings in their feet as they slowly walk up and down. Bodily movements are coarser and less elusive than movements of mind, and confused types will find them easier to apprehend as objects of attention.

To minimise their internal confusion, a teacher will advise confused students to take steps to tackle the external symptoms. If they learn to keep themselves and their environment clean and tidy, they'll find their efforts on the physical level feed directly back into the world of the mind; many have been surprised at the difference such a simple instruction can make. The teacher will also suggest that they try to keep their attention on whatever task they're currently performing, rather than allowing it to drift where it will. He may further recommend that they have a room with a view – otherwise they'll tend to get lost within themselves and may find it difficult to relate to anyone or anything external.

Speculative types, on the other hand, will be advised to opt for a room with no view whatsoever – no windows at all, preferably. The more sensory stimulation they have available, the more readily will they spin off into a proliferation of ideas and concepts. Narrow down their visual field and they may actually begin to look at their craving for stimulation and for speculative thinking in a meditative manner, rather than blindly indulging it.

The mental world of the speculator – both in and out of the meditation – can be described, in a word, as lively. He's constantly thinking, planning, analysing. His ideal is to experience an endless succession of new and exciting mental stimuli.

His meditation teacher will accordingly advise him to restrain his thinking – to learn to gather data by simply observing his experience, rather than continually thinking about his experience. Once the speculator has learned to discipline his mind, he'll find its natural curiosity and openness real assets in his quest for understanding.

One primary task in meditation is learning what not to do – learning to identify and restrain inefficient behaviour, the kind of mental actions deriving from the three negative roots. Consequently there is much that needs to be said about the approach of the negative roots to the spiritual path and about the problems cravers, hate types and confused types experience with meditation. When the positive roots predominate, however, the mind is less troubled and consequently it is in a fit state to develop the necessary meditative qualities. In the case of the faith, intelligent and speculative types there are fewer obstacles cluttering the mind and therefore they can apply themselves to the practice with greater facility. As much of meditation instruction is concerned with overcoming obstacles and hindrances, there's less to be said about their meditation.

Note that the positive roots are not free from suffering – the Buddha said that *all* conditioned things are unsatisfactory – including efficient actions. The cultivation of positive qualities will ensure the best possible life in the world but that on its own cannot completely free one from suffering. It's definitely the case, however, that changing the balance of the mind from predominantly negative to predominantly positive is an essential prerequisite for developing the insight which will ultimately lead beyond efficiency and inefficiency altogether.

Where cravers will collect more of anything, **faith types** collect more of the right things – right meditation practices, right ways of living, right books to study, right people to learn from. Faith types delight in practices such as service and generosity. Their goal is to develop fully such positive qualities as love and compassion. They can't get enough of spiritual teachings and will do their best to put themselves in an environment where they've got constant access to them.

Faith types are very easy to teach as they simply absorb instructions; they drink them in without a shadow of resistance. If they find a good teacher they're unstoppable. They don't take time out to mull over possible pros and cons but simply put their instructions straight into practice. Should their teacher tell them to jump off the roof they would do so, confident that any such order would only be given with their own best interests in mind.

When faith is strong, the meditation practice is often characterised by a sense of joy, a conviction that whatever the ups and downs everything is moving in a positive direction and all is well with the world.

If the faith type has a drawback, it's that he tends not to discriminate enough. Taking everything on trust, he just lets it all flow through, and a teacher may advise that he sharpens up the analytical side of the mind, noting exactly what's present and how all the pieces link together.

The intelligent type, on the other hand, can be a master of discrimination. Recognising what is efficient and what is not, he endeavours to remove all hindrances to progress and tries to do so in a sensible and balanced manner. Where the hate type goes for force, the intelligent type knows the value of patient repetition and is willing to turn his attention back to the meditation object time and time again – as often as it takes for the mind to settle down.

To the teacher, an intelligent type is a desirable student as he's always ready to be corrected and advised. He naturally tends to gravitate towards a middle way and thus rarely needs to be warned to avoid the extremes. Aware that meditation cannot be isolated from life itself, that each moment offers an opportunity to find the answers he seeks, he'll be quick to grasp the importance of practising mindfulness throughout the day.

The one possible failing of the intelligent type is that he tends to be too controlling. He believes progress lies in a continual refinement of his approach as he discards ever more subtle levels of inefficiency. Unfortunately his view that he can somehow produce enlightenment through his own efforts is flawed – reality is not answerable to personal will.

19

BEYOND CHARACTER ANALYSIS

Through meditation, we can train in a capacity for awareness, for becoming conscious of our experience as it occurs. We can become increasingly conscious not only of our physical and verbal behaviour but also of the kinds of mental actions we choose to make. Once we know what's going on in our minds, we can more easily take steps to change the way we behave.

Through the guidance of a competent teacher and our own observations of experience, we will learn that actions associated with the roots of craving, hatred and confusion invariably and inevitably lead to distress, and we can set about restraining them. We can refuse to indulge our habitual tendencies, whether they be craving-based, like greed, jealousy and deceit; hatred-based like envy or anger; or confusion-based, like agitation, worry and indecision.

As our understanding of our own natures grows, as we begin to realise that we do have a choice in what we do, say and think, we find that we prefer to abandon inefficient modes of behaviour and life becomes accordingly smoother and less distressing. This increasing calmness provides an essential foundation for the successful pursuit of the spiritual path.

As well as restraining behaviour based on the negative roots, it's usually the case that we also need to strengthen the positive roots within our make-up. Having learned to keep in check our tendency to critical and resentful thinking, for example, we can then set about training in the efficient characteristic of loving-kindness (*metta*) by consciously turning our attention to the good points in people rather than picking always on their faults.

Dependent on which root is strongest within us, we may pursue the search for understanding from the devotional approach of the faith type, the discriminative approach of the intelligent type or the investigative approach of the speculator. Each of these approaches is equally valid. In fact, all three of the positive roots are necessary in some degree. As Alan James has said: 'You need speculation – to provide a line of enquiry, to ask "What's it all about?"; you need faith – that there is an answer to be found; and unquestionably you need intelligence – to discard the unworkable solutions.'

But the final answer cannot lie in the perfection of these positive roots. Underlying each one of the six roots – whether positive or negative – is a fundamental ignorance about the nature of reality. Every unenlightened individual wants to change things – whether their environments or their own characters – and this applies as much to the positive roots as it does to the negative. Dissatisfied with what is, we desire things to be different from the way they are; we crave. And as the second noble truth of Buddhism makes clear, that craving always leads to suffering.

Again to quote Alan James: 'None of these six roots can see that things as they are – right now, right here – are perfect. There is nothing that is wrong, there is nothing that is missing. It is complete, total and absolutely perfect here and now, always. And our very desire to look elsewhere, to improve the quality of life, is the thing that ensures that there is discontent, unsatisfactoriness and unhappiness.'

* * *

One term the Buddha often used in describing his teaching was *ehi-passiko* – literally, 'come and see'. It points to the fact that he did not ask his students simply to accept his words in blind faith but rather expected them to test out his teaching against their own experience.

Buddhist character analysis being one of the many facets of the legacy the Buddha left the world, it too can be described as *ehi-passiko* – it's a system that requires us to test it out for ourselves. It's not a theoretical approach to the subject but one that is solidly grounded on experience, on the observations we make about ourselves and other people. And whilst it may at first seem deceptively simple, the more we learn about it, the more we realise how complex and profound it actually is.

The human personality is dynamic, it's constantly in flux. Sometimes our actions will be motivated by hatred, sometimes by faith, sometimes by intelligence. Our style of dress may be symptomatic of craving, the manner in which we work may indicate a state of confusion. The root that dominates our behaviour may change from month to month, day to day, moment to moment. Nevertheless, taking the whole picture into consideration, one or maybe two roots will manifest more frequently than the rest, and to identify the predominant root in ourselves and in other people can bring us considerable benefits.

Observing how the roots permeate all aspects of behaviour – mental, verbal and physical – we come to appreciate the depth and subtlety of this system. Our understanding of human nature is considerably enhanced and much of the distress entailed in relating with people is smoothed out of our lives.

If we choose to go further, we can utilise this increased sense of calm and ease as an essential step on the road to the beyond – we can restrain craving, hatred and confusion; we can cultivate faith, intelligence and speculation; and by developing understanding of the true nature of reality, we can finally transcend them all.

These books are available by mail-order:

Buddhist Character Analysis	£6.95
The Unfolding of Wisdom	
softback	£8.95
hardback	£10.95
Modern Buddhism	£7.95
Life as a Siamese Monk	£8.95

(Prices include postage and packing)

Please send to:

Aukana Trust
9 Masons Lane
Bradford on Avon
Wiltshire BA15 1QN

MODERN BUDDHISM Alan & Jacqui James

Presenting timeless truths in a 20th-century context, *Modern Buddhism* provides answers to questions that have always haunted mankind. Death and dying: a wasted and terrifying experience – or an opportunity for spiritual growth? A meditation teacher describes the way she helped her mother approach the doors of death. Family relationships: why do some families live in harmony, whilst other are constantly at war? Sexuality: what sexual habits are most conducive to progress along the path? Alan & Jacqui James belong to the tradition of teachers who present the essence of Buddhism in a way which is totally in tune with the needs of their own time and culture.

In a confused and dark world, the book is like a ray of light showing the path to sanity and peace – **Buddhism Today, Brisbane**

ISBN 0 9511769 1 9   215 x 135mm   176 pages

LIFE AS A SIAMESE MONK Richard Randall

May 1954, Bangkok – 10,000 people converge on the outlying temple of Wat Paknam to witness an historic ceremony. 47-year-old journalist Richard Randall is taking the saffron robe to ordain as a Buddhist monk. Known henceforth as Kapilavaddho Bhikkhu, he is the first Englishman to enter the monkhood in Thailand. After an intensive meditation training and some remarkable experiences in concentration and insight practice, Kapilavaddho later went on to play a key role in the introduction of Buddhist meditation to the West.

An exceptionally fine Dhamma-read – **Buddhism Now**

An inspiring story of Buddhist devotion – **Light of Peace, Bangkok**

ISBN 0 9511769 2 7   230 x 150mm   224 pages + 8 pages photos

Other books available from Aukana:

THE UNFOLDING OF WISDOM
The Buddha's Path to Enlightenment
Alan James

'... it is like having lived all your life in a dark cave, never being sure where the walls, the ceiling or the exits were, never being sure of the real shape of the space around you. When at last you bring in some light to the darkness, immediately your old idea of the cave disappears. The illumination of true vision eliminates what had been total darkness, including all your speculations about the reality of the cave.

'When this occurs, there is never any need to refer to your earlier idea of how things were; it simply becomes irrelevant. Now you know things as they are. What interest can speculative fantasies have for you now?'

The Unfolding of Wisdom is uncompromising. It presents the facts about spiritual progress. It is not for those who would speculate about symbolism or metaphor but for those who would dare to approach truth directly.

ISBN 0 9511769 4 3 (hardback) 0 9511769 5 1 (softback)
230 x 155mm   224 pages

All profits from the sale of this book go directly to the Aukana Trust, a registered charity (No 326938) dedicated to the promotion of the Buddha's teaching.

Under the spiritual guidance of Alan James, the Aukana Trust provides a wide range of facilities, from introductory evening classes in meditation and Buddhist philosophy right through to full-time monastic training. Most of the activities are held at the House of Inner Tranquillity in Bradford on Avon but the Trust also runs classes in London and Oxford.

If you would like more details please write to:

Aukana Trust
9 Masons Lane
Bradford on Avon
Wiltshire BA15 1QN
England